# Official IELTS Practice M

# Contents

A CD containing the Practice Listening test and three sample candidate Speaking tests is included at the back of this booklet.

# Introduction

These Practice Materials are intended to give IELTS candidates an idea of what the test is like. They also give candidates the opportunity to test themselves to see whether their English is at the level required to take IELTS.

Please note, however, that a high score on these Practice Materials does not guarantee that the same standard will be reached in the real IELTS test.

**These Practice Materials are approved by the British Council, Cambridge ESOL and IDP: IELTS Australia.**

# Format of the IELTS Test

The IELTS test is made up of four components. All candidates take the same Listening and Speaking tests. There is a choice of Reading and Writing tests depending on whether you are an **ACADEMIC** or **GENERAL TRAINING** candidate.

The tests are normally taken in the order Listening, Reading, Writing, Speaking, and are timed as follows:

| | |
|---|---|
| Listening | approximately 30 minutes |
| Reading | 60 minutes |
| Writing | 60 minutes |
| Speaking | 11–14 minutes |

Information on the test format can be found in *IELTS Information for Candidates*. This is available from test centres or can be downloaded from the IELTS website **www.ielts.org**

The website also contains further information on the test content, test administration and marking procedures.

# How to use the Practice Test

## Preparing to take the Practice Test

1  Decide which Reading and Writing tests you should take – **ACADEMIC** or **GENERAL TRAINING**.

The Academic module assesses the English language skills required for academic study or professional recognition.

The emphasis of the General Training module is on language skills in broad social and workplace contexts. It is suitable for candidates who are going to migrate to an English-speaking country (Australia, Canada, New Zealand, UK). It is also suitable for candidates planning to undertake work experience or training programmes not at degree level, or to complete their secondary education.

2  You need to write your answers on the answer sheets. The Listening/Reading answer sheets are on pages 80–81. Instructions on how to complete the Listening/Reading answer sheets are on page 79. The Writing answer booklet is on pages 82–85. You may photocopy the answer sheets/booklets so that they may be reused.

3  Prepare for the Practice Test carefully:

- Find a quiet room with a table to write on.

- Make sure that you are not going to be interrupted.

- Make sure that you have everything you need, i.e. pencils, pens, an eraser, a pencil sharpener and a CD player for the Listening test.

- Make sure you have a watch or clock. It is essential that you follow the time allowed for each component. There is a lot of material in the Reading and Writing tests and one of the aims of this Practice Test is to see how you can manage in the time allowed. **If you allow yourself longer than the test says, you will not get a true picture of your ability.**

## Taking the Practice Test

1  Turn to the **Listening test** on page 5. Do not open it yet. Put the Listening test CD in the CD player. Do not play it yet.

Read the instructions on the cover of the question paper and make sure you understand them. Start the Listening test CD. Note that once you have started the CD, you must not stop it. You must let it run straight through to the end. It will take about 30 minutes. You should write your answers as you listen in the spaces provided next to the questions on the question paper.

Once the recording has ended, do not listen to it again.

Copy your answers carefully into the corresponding boxes on the answer sheet. For example, write the answer to question 1 in box 1. You must copy your answers onto the answer sheet in 10 minutes.

2  Now turn to the appropriate **Reading test** (Academic or General Training) on pages 14 or 37. Read the instructions on the cover of the question paper and make sure you understand them. Make a note of the time and start the test.

You may write your answers directly on the answer sheet, or you may write your answers on the question paper and then copy them onto the answer sheet. Note, however, that no extra time is allowed for copying answers onto the answer sheet.

After 60 minutes, stop immediately.

3  Allow yourself a short break.

4  Now turn to the appropriate **Writing test** (Academic or General Training). There are three examples of the Academic Writing test on pages 28–36. There are two examples of the General Training Writing test on pages 49–54.

Read the instructions on the cover of the question paper. Once you are sure you understand them, make a note of the time and start the test.

Write your answers in the Writing answer booklet.

You should spend approximately 20 minutes on Task 1, and approximately 40 minutes on Task 2.

After 60 minutes, stop immediately.

5  Allow yourself a break.

6  There is information about the **Speaking test** and sample Speaking materials on pages 55–56.

Read through this material and practise making responses.

## Marking the Practice Test

1  Read 'How to mark the Listening and Reading Practice Tests' on page 57, and then check your answers to the Listening and Reading tests against those in the answer keys on page 58.

To interpret your Listening and Reading scores, read 'Interpreting your Scores' on page 62.

2  You cannot mark the Writing test yourself, but you will have a clearer idea of what is required in the time allowed. There is information on how Writing is assessed on page 63.

You will find sample answers to the Writing tasks on pages 64–76. Each answer has been given a Band Score and these are explained by examiner comments.

3  You cannot mark your speaking performance using the sample Speaking test materials, but there is information on how Speaking is assessed on page 77. On the CD, there are three sample Speaking tests. On page 78, there are Band Scores and examiner comments for each sample candidate performance.

## Taking the Practice Test again

1   If your scores on the Practice Test are low and you decide to have more English lessons or study to improve a language skill, you may want to take the test again to see if you have made progress before you apply to take IELTS. You should, therefore, put the Practice Materials away and not refer to them until you are ready to try again. If you do this, there is a good chance that you will have forgotten the answers and that the Practice Test will still give you a reasonable indication of the score you would get on IELTS. You should therefore not re-take the Practice Test too soon after first taking it.

2   Please note that the Practice Materials are not designed to measure short-term progress. If you re-take the Practice Test too soon, you may find that your scores are no higher than they were.

Candidate Name _____

Candidate Number
[                    ]

# INTERNATIONAL ENGLISH LANGUAGE TESTING SYSTEM  0380/4
# 0381/4

Listening

**PRACTICE MATERIALS**                    Approximately 30 minutes

Additional materials:
Answer sheet for Listening and Reading

**Time**    Approximately 30 minutes (plus 10 minutes' transfer time)

## INSTRUCTIONS TO CANDIDATES

Do not open this question paper until you are told to do so.

**Write your name and candidate number in the spaces at the top of this page.**

Listen to the instructions for each part of the paper carefully.

Answer all the questions.

While you are listening, write your answers on the question paper.

You will have 10 minutes at the end of the test to copy your answers onto the separate answer sheet. Use a pencil.

At the end of the test, hand in this question paper.

## INFORMATION FOR CANDIDATES

There are **four** parts to the test.

You will hear each part **once** only.

There are **40** questions.

Each question carries one mark.

For each part of the test, there will be time for you to look through the questions and time for you to check your answers.

---

●● **BRITISH**
●● **COUNCIL**

**IELTS**
**AUSTRALIA**

**UNIVERSITY** *of* **CAMBRIDGE**
ESOL Examinations

PV7

© UCLES 2009

# SECTION 1    *Questions 1 – 10*

*Questions 1 and 2*

*Choose the correct letter, A, B or C.*

> *Example*
>
> Penny's interview took place
>
> A    yesterday.
> B    last week.
> C    two weeks ago.

**1**    What kind of shop is it?

　　　　A    a ladies' dress shop
　　　　B    a department store
　　　　C    a children's clothes shop

**2**    What is the name of the section Penny will be working in?

　　　　A    the Youngster
　　　　B    the Youngset
　　　　C    the Young Set

Questions 3 – 10

Complete the notes below.

Write **NO MORE THAN TWO WORDS AND/OR A NUMBER** for each answer.

| | |
|---|---|
| **Pay:** | $6.50 an hour |
| **Breaks:** | one hour for lunch and **3** ..................... coffee breaks |
| **Holidays:** | three weeks a year in the first two years |
| | four weeks a year in the **4** ..................... |
| **Staff training:** | held on the **5** ..................... of every month |
| **Special staff benefits or 'perks':** | staff discount of **6** ..................... on everything except sale goods |
| **Information on pension:** | see Personnel Manager, office in **7** ..................... |
| **Boss's name:** | **8** ..................... |
| **Duties:** | serve customers |
| | **9** ..................... |
| | check for shoplifters |
| | check the stock |
| **Expected to wear:** | a **10** ..................... , a red blouse, and a name badge |

**Turn over ▶**

## SECTION 2          *Questions 11 – 20*

*Questions 11 – 13*

*Choose the correct letter, **A**, **B** or **C**.*

11      The Bridge Hotel is located in

      **A**      the city centre.
      **B**      the country.
      **C**      the suburbs.

12      The newest sports facility in the hotel is

      **A**      a swimming pool.
      **B**      a fitness centre.
      **C**      a tennis court.

13      The hotel restaurant specialises in

      **A**      healthy food.
      **B**      local food.
      **C**      international food.

*Questions 14 and 15*

*Choose **TWO** letters, **A-E**.*

Which **TWO** business facilities are mentioned?

      **A**      internet access
      **B**      mobile phone hire
      **C**      audio-visual facilities
      **D**      airport transport
      **E**      translation services

Questions 16 – 20

Complete the table below.

Write **NO MORE THAN TWO WORDS AND/OR A NUMBER** for each answer.

| SHORT BREAK PACKAGES | | |
|---|---|---|
| **Length of stay** | **Cost (per person per night)** | **Special features** |
| 2 days | **16** £ ..................... | Full cooked breakfast<br><br>Entertainment in the **17** ..................... |
| 3 days | £60 | As above, plus:<br><br>– a **18** ..................... |
| 5 days | **19** £ ..................... | As above, plus:<br><br>– free beauty therapy on two of the days<br><br>– full-day membership of a **20** ..................... |

**Turn over ▶**

## SECTION 3          *Questions 21 – 30*

*Questions 21 and 22*

*Complete the sentences below.*

*Write **NO MORE THAN TWO WORDS** for each answer.*

### Research Project

- Harry and Katy have to concentrate on coastal change for their next project.

**21**     Their work could be delayed by the ...................... .

- They plan to get help from the Marine Biology Unit.

**22**     Before they go to the beach, they need to visit the ...................... .

*Questions 23 – 26*

Who will do each of the following tasks?

| | |
|---|---|
| **A** | Katy |
| **B** | Harry |
| **C** | Both Katy and Harry |

*Write the correct letter, **A**, **B** or **C**, next to questions 23-26.*

**Tasks**

**23**     take photographs     .........

**24**     collect samples     .........

**25**     interview people     .........

**26**     analyse data     .........

*Questions 27 – 30*

*Choose the correct letter, **A**, **B** or **C**.*

**27**    Why does Harry want to do the presentation?

      **A**      to practise skills for his future career
      **B**      to catch up with his course requirements
      **C**      to get a better mark than for his last presentation

**28**    What is Katy's attitude to writing up the project?

      **A**      She is worried about the time available for writing.
      **B**      She thinks it is unfair if she has to do all the writing.
      **C**      She is concerned that some parts will be difficult.

**29**    Why does Harry want to involve the other students at the end of the presentation?

      **A**      to get their opinions about the conclusions
      **B**      to help him and Katy reach firm conclusions
      **C**      to see if they have reached similar conclusions

**30**    Katy agrees to deal with any questions because

      **A**      she feels she will be confident about the material.
      **B**      Harry will be doing the main presentation.
      **C**      she has already told Dr Smith she will do this.

**Turn over ▶**

## SECTION 4    Questions 31 – 40

*Questions 31 – 33*

*Complete the sentences below.*

*Write **NO MORE THAN THREE WORDS** for each answer.*

### Peregrine Falcons

31    The Peregrine falcons found in ………………… are not migratory birds.

32    There is disagreement about their maximum ………………… .

33    When the female is guarding the nest, the male spends most of his time ………………… .

*Questions 34 – 37*

*Complete the table below.*

*Write **NO MORE THAN THREE WORDS** for each answer.*

| Age of falcons | What occurs |
|---|---|
| 20 days old | The falcons **34** ………………… |
| 28 days old | The falcons are **35** ………………… |
| 2 months old | The falcons **36** ………………… permanently |
| 1-12 months old | More than half of falcons **37** ………………… |

*Questions 38 – 40*

*Complete the notes below.*

*Write **NO MORE THAN THREE WORDS** for each answer.*

## Procedures used for field research on Peregrine falcon chicks

First:      catch chicks

Second:   **38** ...................... to legs

Third:     **39** ..................... of chicks

Fourth:    take blood sample to assess level of pesticide

Fifth:     check the **40** ..................... of the birds

Candidate Name _____  Candidate Number [          ]

## INTERNATIONAL ENGLISH LANGUAGE TESTING SYSTEM  **0381/1**

Academic Reading

**PRACTICE MATERIALS**                                        1 hour

Additional materials:
    Answer sheet for Listening and Reading

**Time**    1 hour

## INSTRUCTIONS TO CANDIDATES

Do not open this question paper until you are told to do so.

**Write your name and candidate number in the spaces at the top of this page.**

Read the instructions for each part of the paper carefully.

Answer all the questions.

Write your answers on the answer sheet. Use a pencil.

You **must** complete the answer sheet within the time limit.

At the end of the test, hand in both this question paper and your answer sheet.

## INFORMATION FOR CANDIDATES

There are **40** questions on this question paper.

Each question carries one mark.

  UNIVERSITY *of* CAMBRIDGE
ESOL Examinations

PV1

© UCLES 2009

## READING PASSAGE 1

*You should spend about 20 minutes on **Questions 1-13**, which are based on Reading Passage 1 on pages 2 and 3.*

# Spider silk cuts weight of bridges

*A strong, light bio-material made by genes from spiders could transform construction and industry*

**A**  Scientists have succeeded in copying the silk-producing genes of the *Golden Orb Weaver* spider and are using them to create a synthetic material which they believe is the model for a new generation of advanced bio-materials. The new material, biosilk, which has been spun for the first time by researchers at DuPont, has an enormous range of potential uses in construction and manufacturing.

**B**  The attraction of the silk spun by the spider is a combination of great strength and enormous elasticity, which man-made fibres have been unable to replicate. On an equal-weight basis, spider silk is far stronger than steel and it is estimated that if a single strand could be made about 10m in diameter, it would be strong enough to stop a jumbo jet in flight. A third important factor is that it is extremely light. Army scientists are already looking at the possibilities of using it for lightweight, bullet-proof vests and parachutes.

**C**  For some time, biochemists have been trying to synthesise the drag-line silk of the *Golden Orb Weaver*. The drag-line silk, which forms the radial arms of the web, is stronger than the other parts of the web and some biochemists believe a synthetic version could prove to be as important a material as nylon, which has been around for 50 years, since the discoveries of Wallace Carothers and his team ushered in the age of polymers.

**D**  To recreate the material, scientists, including Randolph Lewis at the University of Wyoming, first examined the silk-producing gland of the spider. 'We took out the glands that produce the silk and looked at the coding for the protein material they make, which is spun into a web. We then went looking for clones with the right DNA,' he says.

**E**     At DuPont, researchers have used both yeast and bacteria as hosts to grow the raw material, which they have spun into fibres. Robert Dorsch, DuPont's director of biochemical development, says the globules of protein, comparable with marbles in an egg, are harvested and processed. 'We break open the bacteria, separate out the globules of protein and use them as the raw starting material. With yeast, the gene system can be designed so that the material excretes the protein outside the yeast for better access,' he says.

**F**     'The bacteria and the yeast produce the same protein, equivalent to that which the spider uses in the drag lines of the web. The spider mixes the protein into a water-based solution and then spins it into a solid fibre in one go. Since we are not as clever as the spider and we are not using such sophisticated organisms, we substituted man-made approaches and dissolved the protein in chemical solvents, which are then spun to push the material through small holes to form the solid fibre.'

**G**     Researchers at DuPont say they envisage many possible uses for a new biosilk material. They say that earthquake-resistant suspension bridges hung from cables of synthetic spider silk fibres may become a reality. Stronger ropes, safer seat belts, shoe soles that do not wear out so quickly and tough new clothing are among the other applications. Biochemists such as Lewis see the potential range of uses of biosilk as almost limitless. 'It is very strong and retains elasticity; there are no man-made materials that can mimic both these properties. It is also a biological material with all the advantages that has over petrochemicals,' he says.

**H**     At DuPont's laboratories, Dorsch is excited by the prospect of new super-strong materials but he warns they are many years away. 'We are at an early stage but theoretical predictions are that we will wind up with a very strong, tough material, with an ability to absorb shock, which is stronger and tougher than the man-made materials that are conventionally available to us,' he says.

**I**     The spider is not the only creature that has aroused the interest of material scientists. They have also become envious of the natural adhesive secreted by the sea mussel. It produces a protein adhesive to attach itself to rocks. It is tedious and expensive to extract the protein from the mussel, so researchers have already produced a synthetic gene for use in surrogate bacteria.

**Turn over ▶**

Questions 1 – 5

Reading Passage 1 has nine paragraphs, **A-I**.

Which paragraph contains the following information?

*Write the correct letter, **A-I**, in boxes 1-5 on your answer sheet.*

1       a comparison of the ways two materials are used to replace silk-producing glands

2       predictions regarding the availability of the synthetic silk

3       ongoing research into other synthetic materials

4       the research into the part of the spider that manufactures silk

5       the possible application of the silk in civil engineering

Questions 6 – 10

*Complete the flow-chart below.*

*Choose **NO MORE THAN TWO WORDS** from the passage for each answer.*

*Write your answers in boxes 6-10 on your answer sheet.*

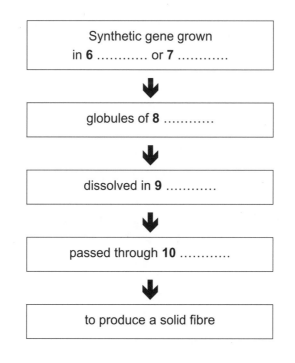

Synthetic gene grown in **6** ………… or **7** …………

⬇

globules of **8** …………

⬇

dissolved in **9** …………

⬇

passed through **10** …………

⬇

to produce a solid fibre

Questions 11 – 13

Do the following statements agree with the information given in Reading Passage 1?

In boxes 11-13 on your answer sheet, write

| | |
|---|---|
| **TRUE** | if the statement agrees with the information |
| **FALSE** | if the statement contradicts the information |
| **NOT GIVEN** | if there is no information on this |

11    Biosilk has already replaced nylon in parachute manufacture.

12    The spider produces silk of varying strengths.

13    Lewis and Dorsch co-operated in the synthetic production of silk.

**Turn over ▶**

**READING PASSAGE 2**

*You should spend about 20 minutes on* **Questions 14-26**, *which are based on Reading Passage 2 on pages 6 and 7.*

# Revolutions in Mapping

Today, the mapmaker's vision is no longer confined to what the human eye can see. The perspective of mapmaking has shifted from the crow's nest of the sailing vessel, mountain top and airplane to new orbital heights. Radar, which bounces microwave radio signals off a given surface to create images of its contours and textures, can penetrate jungle foliage and has produced the first maps of the mountains of the planet Venus. And a combination of sonar and radar produces charts of the seafloor, putting much of Earth on the map for the first time. 'Suddenly it's a whole different world for us,' says Joel Morrison, chief of geography at the U.S. Bureau of the Census. 'Our future as mapmakers – even ten years from now – is uncertain.'

The world's largest collection of maps resides in the basement of the Library of Congress in Washington, D.C. The collection, consisting of up to 4.6 million map sheets and 63,000 atlases, includes magnificent bound collections of elaborate maps – the pride of the golden age of Dutch cartography*. In the reading room scholars, wearing thin cotton gloves to protect the fragile sheets, examine ancient maps with magnifying glasses. Across the room people sit at their computer screens, studying the latest maps. With their prodigious memories, computers are able to store data about people, places and environments – the stuff of maps – and almost instantly information is displayed on the screen in the desired geographic context, and at the click of a button, a print-out of the map appears.

Measuring the spherical Earth ranks as the first major milestone in scientific cartography. This was first achieved by the Greek astronomer Eratosthenes, a scholar at the famous Alexandrian Library in Egypt in the third century BC. He calculated the Earth's circumference as 25,200 miles, which was remarkably accurate. The longitudinal circumference is known today to be 24,860 miles.

Building on the ideas of his predecessors, the astronomer and geographer Ptolemy, working in the second century AD, spelled out a system for organising maps according to grids of latitude and longitude. Today, parallels of latitude are often spaced at intervals of 10 to 20 degrees and meridians** at 15 degrees, and this is the basis for the width of modern time zones. Another legacy of Ptolemy's is his advice to cartographers to create maps to scale. Distance on today's maps is expressed as a fraction or ratio of the real distance. But mapmakers in Ptolemy's time lacked the geographic knowledge to live up to Ptolemy's scientific principles. Even now, when surveyors achieve accuracies down to inches and satellites can plot potential missile targets within feet, maps are not true pictures of reality.

* cartography: mapmaking
** meridians: lines of longitude on the earth running north to south

However, just as the compass improved navigation and created demand for useful charts, so the invention of the printing press in the 15th century put maps in the hands of more people, and took their production away from monks, who had tended to illustrate theology rather than geography. Ocean-going ships launched an age of discovery, enlarging both what could and needed to be mapped, and awakened an intellectual spirit and desire for knowledge of the world.

Inspired by the rediscovered Ptolemy, whose writing had been preserved by Arabs after the sacking of the Alexandrian Library in AD 931, mapmakers in the 15th century gradually replaced theology with knowledge of faraway places, as reported by travelling merchants like Marco Polo.

Gerhardus Mercator, the foremost shipmaker of the 16th century, developed a technique of arranging meridians and parallels in such a way that navigators could draw straight lines between two points and steer a constant compass course between them. This distortion formula, introduced on his world map of 1569, created the 'Greenland problem'. Even on some standard maps to this day, Greenland looks as large as South America – one of the many problems when one tries to portray a round world on a flat sheet of paper. But the Mercator projection was so practical that it is still popular with sailors.

Scientific mapping of the land came into its own with the achievements of the Cassini family – father, son, grandson and great-grandson. In the late 17th century, the Italian-born founder, Jean-Dominique, invented a complex method of determining longitude based on observations of Jupiter's moons. Using this technique, surveyors were able to produce an accurate map of France. The family continued to map the French countryside and his great-grandson finally published their famous Cassini map in 1793 during the French Revolution. While it may have lacked the artistic appeal of earlier maps, it was the model of a social and geographic map showing roads, rivers, canals, towns, abbeys, vineyards, lakes and even windmills. With this achievement, France became the first country to be completely mapped by scientific methods.

Mapmaking has come a long way since those days. Today's surveyors rarely go into the field without being linked to navigation satellites. Their hand-held receivers are the most familiar of the new mapping technologies, and the satellite system, developed and still operated by the US Defense Department, is increasingly used by surveyors. Even ordinary hikers, sailors and explorers can tap into it for data telling them where they are. Simplified civilian versions of the receivers are available for a few hundred dollars and they are also the heart of electronic map displays available in some cars. Cartography is pressing on to cosmic frontiers, but its objective is, and always has been, to communicate a sense of 'here' in relation to 'there', however far away 'there' may be.

Turn over ▶

*Questions 14 – 18*

*Choose the correct letter, **A**, **B**, **C** or **D**.*

*Write the correct letter in boxes 14-18 on your answer sheet.*

**14**    According to the first paragraph, mapmakers in the 21ˢᵗ century

    **A**    combine techniques to chart unknown territory.
    **B**    still rely on being able to see what they map.
    **C**    are now able to visit the darkest jungle.
    **D**    need input from experts in other fields.

**15**    The Library of Congress offers an opportunity to

    **A**    borrow from their collection of Dutch maps.
    **B**    learn how to restore ancient and fragile maps.
    **C**    enjoy the atmosphere of the reading room.
    **D**    create individual computer maps to order.

**16**    Ptolemy alerted his contemporaries to the importance of

    **A**    measuring the circumference of the world.
    **B**    organising maps to reflect accurate ratios of distance.
    **C**    working out the distance between parallels of latitude.
    **D**    accuracy and precision in mapping.

**17**    The invention of the printing press

    **A**    revitalised interest in scientific knowledge.
    **B**    enabled maps to be produced more cheaply.
    **C**    changed the approach to mapmaking.
    **D**    ensured that the work of Ptolemy was continued.

**18**    The writer concludes by stating that

    **A**    mapmaking has become too specialised.
    **B**    cartographers work in very harsh conditions.
    **C**    the fundamental aims of mapmaking remain unchanged.
    **D**    the possibilities of satellite mapping are infinite.

*Questions 19 – 21*

*Look at the following list of achievements (Questions 19-21) and the list of mapmakers below.*

*Match each achievement with the correct mapmaker, A, B, C or D.*

*Write the correct letter, A, B, C or D, in boxes 19-21 on your answer sheet.*

**19**     came very close to accurately measuring the distance round the Earth

**20**     produced maps showing man-made landmarks

**21**     laid the foundation for our modern time zones

> **List of Mapmakers**
>
> **A**     Mercator
> **B**     Ptolemy
> **C**     Cassini family
> **D**     Eratosthenes

*Questions 22 – 26*

*Complete the summary below.*

*Choose **NO MORE THAN TWO WORDS** from the passage for each answer.*

*Write your answers in boxes 22-26 on your answer sheet.*

Ancient maps allow us to see how we have come to make sense of the world. They also reflect the attitudes and knowledge of the day. The first great step in mapmaking took place in **22** ………… in the 3$^{rd}$ century BC. Work continued in this tradition until the 2$^{nd}$ century AD but was then abandoned for over a thousand years, during which time maps were the responsibility of **23** ………… rather than scientists. Fortunately, however, the writings of **24** ………… had been kept, and interest in scientific mapmaking was revived as scholars sought to produce maps, inspired by the accounts of travellers.

These days, **25** ………… are vital to the creation of maps and radar has allowed cartographers to map areas beyond our immediate world. In addition, this high-tech equipment is not only used to map faraway places, but cheaper versions have also been developed for use in **26** ………… .

**Turn over ▶**

## READING PASSAGE 3

*You should spend about 20 minutes on **Questions 27-40**, which are based on Reading Passage 3 on pages 11 and 12.*

*Questions 27 – 31*

Reading Passage 3 has five sections, **A-E**.

*Choose the correct heading for each section from the list of headings below.*

*Write the correct number, **i-vii**, in boxes 27-31 on your answer sheet.*

---

### List of Headings

| | |
|---|---|
| i | An experiment using people who are receiving medical treatment |
| ii | The experiment that convinced all the researchers |
| iii | Medical benefits of hypnosis make scientific proof less important |
| iv | Lack of data leads to opposing views of hypnotism |
| v | The effects of hypnosis on parts of the brain involved in vision |
| vi | Inducing pain through the use of hypnotism |
| vii | Experiments used to support conflicting views |

---

27    Section **A**

28    Section **B**

29    Section **C**

30    Section **D**

31    Section **E**

# Hypnotism – is it real or just a circus trick?

**A** Hypnosis has been shown through a number of rigorously controlled studies to reduce pain, control blood pressure, and even make warts go away. But because very few studies have attempted to define the actual processes involved, most scientists are sceptical of its power and uses. That scepticism has driven David Spiegel, a professor of psychiatry at Stanford University School of Medicine, USA, and other researchers to take a hard look at what happens in the brain during hypnosis.

Among researchers there are two schools of thought. One claims that hypnosis fundamentally alters subjects' state of mind: they enter a trance, which produces changes in brain activity. The other believes that hypnosis is simply a matter of suggestibility and relaxation. Spiegel belongs to the first school and over the years has had a debate with two scientists on the other side, Irving Kirsch, a University of Connecticut psychologist, and Stephen Kosslyn, a Harvard professor.

**B** Kirsch often uses hypnosis in his practice and doesn't deny that it can be effective. 'With hypnosis you do put people in altered states,' he says. 'But you don't need a trance to do it.' To illustrate the point, Kirsch demonstrates how a subject holding a small object on a chain can make it swing in any direction by mere suggestion, the chain responding to minute movements in the tiny muscles of the fingers. 'You don't have to enter a trance for your subconscious and your body to act upon a suggestion,' Kirsch says. 'The reaction is the result of your focusing on moving the chain in a particular direction.'

Spiegel disagrees. One of his best known studies found that when subjects were hypnotised and given suggestions their brain wave patterns changed, indicating that they had entered a trance. In one of his studies, people under hypnosis were told their forearms were numb, then given light electrical shocks to the wrists. They didn't flinch or respond in any way, and their brain waves resembled those of people who experienced a much weaker shock. To Kirsch this still wasn't enough to prove the power of trance, but Stephen Kosslyn was willing to be convinced. Many external factors could have been responsible for the shift in the subjects' state of mind, but Kosslyn wondered, 'Is there really something going on in the brain?'

**C** To find out, Spiegel and Kosslyn decided to collaborate on a study focusing on a part of the brain that is well understood: the circuit which has been found to process the perception of colour. Spiegel and Kosslyn wanted to see if subjects could set off the circuit by visualising colour while under hypnosis. They selected eight people for the experiment conducted at Massachusetts General Hospital. The subjects were put in a scanner and shown a slide with coloured rectangles while their brain activity was mapped. Then they were shown a black and white slide and told to imagine its having colour. Both tasks were then repeated under hypnosis.

The results were striking. When the subjects truly saw the coloured rectangles, the circuit lit up on both sides of the brain; when they only had to imagine the colour, the circuit lit up only in the right hemisphere. Under hypnosis, however, both sides of the brain became active, just as in regular sight; imagination seemed to take on the quality of a hallucination.

**Turn over ▶**

After the experiment, Kosslyn was forced to admit, 'I'm absolutely convinced now that hypnosis can boost what mental imagery does.' But Kirsch remained sceptical, saying, 'The experiments demonstrate that people are experiencing the effects of hypnotic suggestion but don't prove that they are entering a trance.' He also argued that subjects were told to *see* the card in colour when they were hypnotised but only to *imagine* it in colour when they weren't. 'Being told to pretend you're having an experience is different from the suggestion to have the experience.'

D   Spiegel, however, is a clinician first and a scientist second. He believes the most important thing is that doctors recognise the power of hypnosis and start to use it. Working with Elvira Lang, a radiologist at a Harvard Medical Centre, he is testing the use of hypnosis in the operating room just as he and Kosslyn did in the scanner. Spiegel and Lang took 241 patients scheduled for surgery and divided them into three groups. One group received standard care, another standard care with a sympathetic care provider and the third received standard care, a sympathetic care provider and hypnosis. Every 15 minutes the patients were asked to rate their pain and anxiety levels. They were also hooked up to painkilling medication which they could administer to themselves.

On average, Spiegel and Lang found the hypnotised subjects used less medication, experienced less pain and felt far less anxiety than the other two groups. Original results published in *The Lancet* have been further supported by ongoing studies conducted by Lang.

E   Spiegel's investigations into the nature of hypnosis and its effects on the brain continue. However, if hypnosis is ever to work its way into mainstream medicine and everyday use, physicians will need to know there is solid science behind what sounds like mysticism. Only then will their reluctance to using such things as mind over matter be overcome. 'I agree that the medical use of hypnotism should be based on data rather than belief,' says Spiegel, 'but in the end it doesn't really matter *why* it works, as long as it helps our patients.'

Questions 32 – 36

Choose the correct letter, **A**, **B**, **C** or **D**.

Write the correct letter in boxes 32-36 on your answer sheet.

32    Kirsch uses a small object on a chain to demonstrate that

    **A**       inducing a trance is a simple process.
    **B**       responding to a suggestion does not require a trance.
    **C**       muscles respond as a result of a trance.
    **D**       it is difficult to identify a trance.

33    Spiegel disagrees with Kirsch because the subjects in Spiegel's experiment

    **A**       believed what they were told.
    **B**       showed changes in brain activity.
    **C**       responded as expected to shocks.
    **D**       had similar reactions to control subjects.

34    Kosslyn's response to Spiegel's electric shock experiment was to

    **A**       challenge the results because of external factors.
    **B**       work with Kirsch to disprove Spiegel's results.
    **C**       reverse his previous position on trance.
    **D**       accept that Spiegel's ideas might be correct.

35    Spiegel and Kosslyn's experiment was designed to show that hypnosis

    **A**       affects the electrical responses of the brain.
    **B**       could make colour appear as black and white.
    **C**       has an effect on how shapes are perceived.
    **D**       can enhance the subject's imagination.

36    Kirsch thought Spiegel and Kosslyn's results

    **A**       were worthy of further investigation.
    **B**       had nothing to do with hypnotic suggestion.
    **C**       showed that the possibility of trance existed.
    **D**       were affected by the words used in the instructions.

**Turn over ▶**

Questions 37 – 40

Do the following statements agree with the information given in Reading Passage 3?

*In boxes 37-40 on your answer sheet, write*

| | |
|---|---|
| **TRUE** | *if the statement agrees with the information* |
| **FALSE** | *if the statement contradicts the information* |
| **NOT GIVEN** | *if there is no information on this* |

37    Spiegel is more interested in scientific research than medical practice.

38    Patients in the third group in Spiegel and Lang's experiment were easily hypnotised.

39    In Spiegel and Lang's experiment, a smaller amount of painkiller was needed by the hypnotised patients than by the other two groups.

40    Spiegel feels that doctors should use hypnotism only when it is fully understood.

Candidate Name _____

Candidate Number

[        ]

INTERNATIONAL ENGLISH LANGUAGE TESTING SYSTEM    **0381/2**

Academic Writing

**PRACTICE MATERIALS**    **Example 1**                1 hour

Additional materials:
    Writing answer booklet

**Time**    1 hour

**INSTRUCTIONS TO CANDIDATES**

Do not open this question paper until you are told to do so.

**Write your name and candidate number in the spaces at the top of this page.**

Read the instructions for each task carefully.

Answer both of the tasks.

Write at least 150 words for Task 1.

Write at least 250 words for Task 2.

Write your answers in the answer booklet.

Write clearly in pen or pencil. You may make alterations, but make sure your work is easy to read.

At the end of the test, hand in both this question paper and your answer booklet.

**INFORMATION FOR CANDIDATES**

There are **two** tasks on this question paper.

Task 2 contributes twice as much as Task 1 to the Writing score.

PV5

© UCLES 2009

# WRITING TASK 1

You should spend about 20 minutes on this task.

---

*The charts below show the number of Japanese tourists travelling abroad between 1985 and 1995 and Australia's share of the Japanese tourist market.*

*Summarise the information by selecting and reporting the main features, and make comparisons where relevant.*

---

Write at least 150 words.

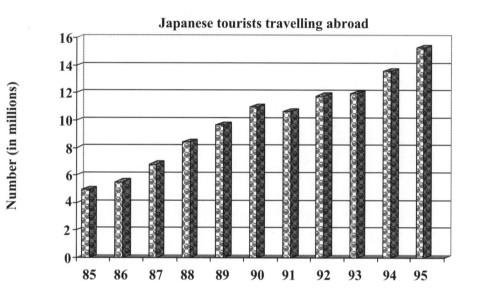

**Japanese tourists travelling abroad**

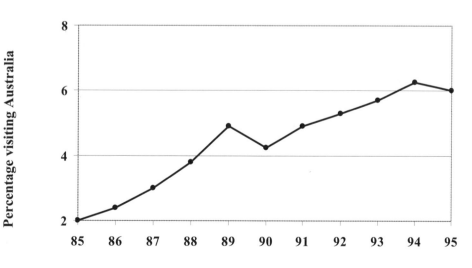

**Australia's share of Japan's tourist market**

## WRITING TASK 2

You should spend about 40 minutes on this task.

Write about the following topic:

*In many countries children are engaged in some kind of paid work. Some people regard this as completely wrong, while others consider it as valuable work experience, important for learning and taking responsibility.*

*Discuss both these views and give your own opinion.*

Give reasons for your answer and include any relevant examples from your own knowledge or experience.

Write at least 250 words.

Candidate Name _____

Candidate Number

[ _____ ]

## INTERNATIONAL ENGLISH LANGUAGE TESTING SYSTEM  **0381/2**

Academic Writing

**PRACTICE MATERIALS**    **Example 2**    1 hour

Additional materials:
    Writing answer booklet

**Time**    1 hour

### INSTRUCTIONS TO CANDIDATES

Do not open this question paper until you are told to do so.

**Write your name and candidate number in the spaces at the top of this page.**

Read the instructions for each task carefully.

Answer both of the tasks.

Write at least 150 words for Task 1.

Write at least 250 words for Task 2.

Write your answers in the answer booklet.

Write clearly in pen or pencil. You may make alterations, but make sure your work is easy to read.

At the end of the test, hand in both this question paper and your answer booklet.

### INFORMATION FOR CANDIDATES

There are **two** tasks on this question paper.

Task 2 contributes twice as much as Task 1 to the Writing score.

**BRITISH COUNCIL**    **IELTS AUSTRALIA**    **UNIVERSITY** *of* **CAMBRIDGE** ESOL Examinations

PV1

© UCLES 2009

## WRITING TASK 1

You should spend about 20 minutes on this task.

> *The diagram below shows the process of using water to produce electricity.*
>
> *Summarise the information by selecting and reporting the main features, and make comparisons where relevant.*

Write at least 150 words.

### Hydro-electric power generation

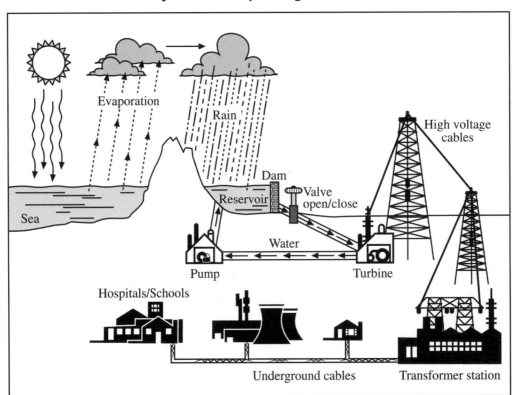

**WRITING TASK 2**

You should spend about 40 minutes on this task.

Write about the following topic:

> *Many old buildings are protected by law because they are part of a nation's history. However, some people think old buildings should be knocked down to make way for new ones because people need houses and offices.*
>
> *How important is it to maintain old buildings?  Should history stand in the way of progress?*

Give reasons for your answer and include any relevant examples from your own knowledge or experience.

Write at least 250 words.

Candidate Name _____

Candidate Number

## INTERNATIONAL ENGLISH LANGUAGE TESTING SYSTEM  **0381/2**

Academic Writing

**PRACTICE MATERIALS**    **Example 3**                          1 hour

Additional materials:
    Writing answer booklet

**Time    1 hour**

## INSTRUCTIONS TO CANDIDATES

Do not open this question paper until you are told to do so.

**Write your name and candidate number in the spaces at the top of this page.**

Read the instructions for each task carefully.

Answer both of the tasks.

Write at least 150 words for Task 1.

Write at least 250 words for Task 2.

Write your answers in the answer booklet.

Write clearly in pen or pencil. You may make alterations, but make sure your work is easy to read.

At the end of the test, hand in both this question paper and your answer booklet.

## INFORMATION FOR CANDIDATES

There are **two** tasks on this question paper.

Task 2 contributes twice as much as Task 1 to the Writing score.

PV3

## WRITING TASK 1

You should spend about 20 minutes on this task.

*The graph below shows the number of complaints made about noise to Environmental Health authorities in the city of Newtown between 1980 and 1996.*

*Summarise the information by selecting and reporting the main features, and make comparisons where relevant.*

Write at least 150 words.

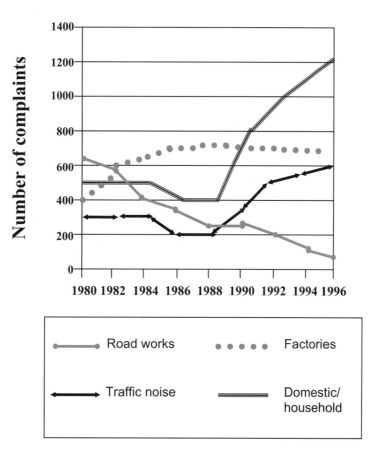

## WRITING TASK 2

You should spend about 40 minutes on this task.

Write about the following topic:

*Television is dangerous because it destroys family life and any sense of community; instead of visiting people or talking with our family we just watch television.*

*To what extent do you agree or disagree with this opinion?*

Give reasons for your answer and include any relevant examples from your own knowledge or experience.

Write at least 250 words.

Candidate Name _____

Candidate Number

## INTERNATIONAL ENGLISH LANGUAGE TESTING SYSTEM  0380/1

General Training Reading

**PRACTICE MATERIALS**                                    1 hour

Additional materials:
    Answer sheet for Listening and Reading

**Time      1 hour**

## INSTRUCTIONS TO CANDIDATES

Do not open this question paper until you are told to do so.

**Write your name and candidate number in the spaces at the top of this page.**

Read the instructions for each part of the paper carefully.

Answer all the questions.

Write your answers on the answer sheet. Use a pencil.

You **must** complete the answer sheet within the time limit.

At the end of the test, hand in both this question paper and your answer sheet.

## INFORMATION FOR CANDIDATES

There are **40** questions on this question paper.

Each question carries one mark.

PV1

## SECTION 1     Questions 1 – 14

*Read the advertisements below and answer Questions 1-4.*

**A**

*Restaurant Supervisor*

*Waiting Staff*

*Telephonist*

———————

*The ideal candidates
must have relevant experience gained in
a high quality hotel. Please call Personnel on
**020-7723-7723**, or send your CV to: The
Aylesbury, Hodge Road, London SE1 8RS*

**The Aylesbury**
LONDON

**B**

USE YOUR
LANGUAGES AND EARN
£450-£1200 P.W.

We are one of the largest business publishers in Europe and have limited vacancies for intelligent young people in our London advertisement sales office. Enquiries from German, Spanish and Eastern European speakers especially welcome. Phone Steve Warburton on 020 7114 9610

**C**

### SECRETARY

Busy Chartered Accountants require experienced/efficient secretary. Accounts experience, proficient typing, and an excellent telephone manner essential; shorthand useful.

**Please send CV to:
Box No. 9246
c/o Weekly Standard
Classified,
9 Berry Street,
Kensington W8 9LP**

**D**

**TRAVEL
COMPANY**

**Vacancy for self-confident person to look after bookings for our Caribbean hotels. Salary based on applicant's experience & suitability. Please send CV to
Greg Taplin, KRI Ltd,
12 Galena Road, London,
W6 3XZ**

**E**

**NANNY WANTED**
for 9 month old handful. Artistic/Prof household Notting Hill, 3 days per week. Some hours flexibility req'd. Knowledge German/Hungarian advantage, not essential 020 7221 6119

**F**

# Hollywood World
LONDON
## Join the Stars!

### Food Servers

The biggest and busiest restaurant in London is seeking additional stars for its team of dedicated professionals. If you have experience in high volume restaurants and are looking for a challenge, then come on down for an audition. **Interview day is on Friday 6th May from 12 noon to 7pm.**

**Hollywood World is located at 29 Foster Street, London W1 6JZ**

*Questions 1 – 4*

*Look at the six job advertisements, **A-F**, on page 2.*

For which advertisement are the following statements true?

*Write the correct letter, **A-F**, in boxes 1-4 on your answer sheet.*

**NB**    *You may use any letter more than once.*

1    Which job is in a hotel?

2    Which job is for someone to look after a child?

3    Which **TWO** advertisements are for waiters?

4    Which **TWO** jobs would be particularly suitable for people who speak a language other than English?

**Turn over ▶**

*Read the text below and answer Questions 5-10.*

# LIST OF TELEPHONE SERVICES

| SERVICE | NUMBER TO DIAL |
|---|---|
| **Operator Services** The operator is there to help you if you have difficulty making a call or if you want to use any of our special call services. These include: ALARM CALLS * ADVICE OF DURATION CHARGE * CREDIT CARD CALLS * FIXED TIME CALLS * FREEFONE CALLS * PERSONAL CALLS * TRANSFERRED CHARGE CALLS * SUBSCRIBER CONTROLLED TRANSFER. For details of charges see our free leaflet. Dial 101 and ask for financial services. | 101 |
| **International Operator** See Section 3 (international) for details. | 123 |
| **Directory Enquiries** Tell the operator the town you require. Have paper and pencil ready. | 142 |
| **International Directory Enquiries** | 130 |
| **Emergency** Tell the operator what service you want. | 010 |
| **Faults** Any fault should be reported to the local fault repair service. | 166 |
| **Sales** For enquiries regarding other purchases. | 170 |
| **Telemessage** If you have something special to say and prefer to say it in writing. | 190 |
| **International Telemessage** | 191 |
| **International Telegrams** You can send a telegram to most other countries. | 192 |
| **Maritime Services** SHIP'S TELEGRAM SERVICE * SHIP'S TELEPHONE SERVICE * INMARSAT SATELLITE SERVICE. You can call or send a message to someone aboard ship by using our Maritime Services. For telephone calls to ships quote the name of the Coast Radio Station if known. For INMARSAT (Maritime Satellite) service dial 178. Give the ship's name, its identification number and ocean region, if known. International Directory Enquiries, code 130, can say if a ship is equipped for satellite service and provide the number. | 200 |
| **Any Other Call Enquiries** | 111 |

*Questions 5 – 10*

*Answer the questions below.*

*Write the correct telephone numbers in boxes 5-10 on your answer sheet.*

**NB**    *You may use any number more than once.*

What number should you dial if

| 5 | there is something wrong with your telephone? |
|---|---|
| 6 | there has been an accident and you want to call an ambulance? |
| 7 | you want to find out a number in a foreign country? |
| 8 | you want to know how much telephone calls cost? |
| 9 | you want to buy an answerphone machine? |
| 10 | you want to use a credit card to pay for a telephone call? |

**Turn over ▶**

*Read the text below and answer Questions 11-14.*

---

# FIRE NOTICE

In the event of fire, the ALARM will ring. On hearing the fire alarm, all those in the West Wing should evacuate the building by staircase J. Rooms 1 to 199 are in the West Wing. All others should use staircase A. The assembly area for occupants of the West Wing is the staff car park at the rear of the building. All others assemble in the courtyard.

Evacuate the building even if the alarm stops.

If you discover a fire, shout "FIRE" and operate the nearest fire alarm. Attack the fire with an extinguisher but do not take any risks. Inform Reception by dialling 3333.

---

*Questions 11 – 14*

*Answer the questions below.*

*Choose **NO MORE THAN THREE WORDS** from the text for each answer.*

*Write your answers in boxes 11-14 on your answer sheet.*

11    You are in room 101. Which staircase should you use to evacuate the building?

12    You are in room 201. Where should you wait outside after evacuating the building?

13    What should you do if the alarm stops?

14    Who should you contact if you discover a fire?

## SECTION 2      *Questions 15 – 27*

*Questions 15 – 21*

The text on page 8 has seven sections, **A-G**.

*Choose the correct heading for each section from the list of headings below.*

*Write the correct number, **i-x**, in boxes 15-21 on your answer sheet.*

---

**List of Headings**

| | |
|---|---|
| i | Standard procedure for disciplinary action |
| ii | Reporting improper activities |
| iii | Relationships with suppliers |
| iv | Inventions and designs |
| v | Company records |
| vi | Confidential information |
| vii | Promoting creativity |
| viii | Respecting media copyright |
| ix | Accessing legal information |
| x | Relationships with competitors |

---

15    Section **A**

16    Section **B**

17    Section **C**

18    Section **D**

19    Section **E**

20    Section **F**

21    Section **G**

**Turn over ▶**

# LGN Energy – Code of Conduct

The purpose of this Code of Conduct is to advise employees of LGN's expectations in respect of conduct, breach of which may lead to investigation and disciplinary action.

**A**     The companies that provide goods and services to LGN Energy are an important resource and should be treated with fairness at all times. Employees should maintain the highest ethical standards in all dealings with them, and managers must act with integrity at all times and lead by example.

**B**     LGN Energy aims to promote its products vigorously in the market place. None of its employees are allowed to collude with rival companies. It is LGN Energy policy to sell products and services on their merits. Therefore the products or services of rival companies should not be criticised.

**C**     Employees should keep accurate, timely and reliable accounts, as these are critical to meeting the financial, legal and management obligations of the company. All reports, invoices and other essential data should be prepared promptly and honestly, and treated with discretion.

**D**     Except as authorised by their manager or required by their duties under their employment contract, employees must not use for their own benefit or gain, or divulge to any person or organisation, any data belonging to the company, or relating to its affairs or dealings, which come to their knowledge during employment.

**E**     Employees should not download or reproduce any material (e.g. music or text) without complying with licensing conditions. Such actions could result in criminal proceedings not only against the company but also against the individual concerned.

**F**     LGN Energy wants to encourage employees to disclose information on any conduct within the company that is causing them concern. If an employee suspects fraud or other behaviour that contravenes this Code of Conduct, they should promptly inform their manager.

**G**     If any employee makes any discoveries or developments capable of being patented during the course of, or in connection with, their employment at LGN, they must tell their manager. All works and intellectual property rights related to their employment will belong to LGN Energy.

*Read the text below and answer Questions 22-27.*

# Maternity Leave

The purpose of this policy is to inform female employees of their entitlement to statutory and company-enhanced maternity rights.

## Antenatal Care

All company employees are entitled to reasonable paid time off during working hours to enable them to receive antenatal care. To qualify, employees are required to produce a certificate from a registered medical practitioner stating that the employee is pregnant, together with an appointment card or other written confirmation of the appointment. However, these requirements do not apply to the first antenatal visit.

Employees are requested to give their immediate manager as much notice as possible and arrange appointments, insofar as is possible, so as not to disrupt the business of the company. Employees will be paid their basic salary in respect of attendance at these appointments.

## Ordinary Maternity Leave (OML)

All employees, irrespective of their length of service, qualify for 26 weeks' OML. An employee must notify the company no later than 15 weeks prior to her Expected Week of Childbirth (EWC) of the date on which she intends to begin her OML.

An employee is not required to give notification if she is absent due to a pregnancy-related illness, or if the baby is born before the planned date for starting maternity leave. Please note that the employee must notify the company that she has given birth as soon as is reasonably practicable.

## Returning from Maternity Leave

No employee is entitled to return from maternity leave until 2 weeks after the birth of the child. Within 28 days of receiving notification from the employee of the date she intends to start her OML, the company will advise her of the date her leave will end. An employee who intends to return to work at the end of her OML period does not have to notify the company in advance of her return.

If the employee wishes to use any annual leave she has accrued to delay her return, she is obliged to request authorisation from the company at least 28 days before she wishes to take it.

**Turn over ▶**

Questions 22 – 27

Complete the notes below.

Choose **NO MORE THAN THREE WORDS AND/OR A NUMBER** from the text for each answer.

Write your answers in boxes 22-27 on your answer sheet.

## Antenatal Care

- Obtain proof of pregnancy from a **22** ............ and also an appointment card (NB not necessary for first antenatal visit)
- Tell your immediate manager as soon as you can
- You will receive your **23** ............ from your company during antenatal care

## Ordinary Maternity Leave

- Doesn't depend on your **24** ............ (everyone gets same amount of OML)
- Tell your employer at least **25** ............ before EWC about starting date of OML
- No need to tell your employer if you are off work because of **26** ............

## Returning from Maternity Leave

- Cannot return to work until 2 weeks after birth
- No need to notify company if coming back when OML finishes
- Must ask for permission if choosing to postpone return by taking any **27** ............ still owing to you

**SECTION 3**         *Questions 28 – 40*

*Read the text below and answer Questions 28-40.*

# WINTER GAMES

Ice, danger and
                exhilaration

The 17th Winter Games, held in Norway in 1994, were part of an Olympic tradition which goes back almost 3,000 years. For more than 1,000 years the ancient Games were held, every four years, on hallowed ground near Mount Olympus, where the Greek gods were said to live.

The 'Olympics' brought together men from war-torn tribes and states in Greece and its colonies. A sacred truce was declared to allow men to travel to the games in safety. Women could not take part and were forbidden, on pain of death, even to attend the Games.

The ancient Olympics were abolished by the Roman Emperor Theodosius in 393 AD, after Greece had lost its independence. But the idea never died and the Frenchman Baron Pierre de Coubertin, an educator and scholar, founded the modern Olympics. His aim was to bring together, once every four years, athletes from all countries on the friendly fields of amateur sport. No account was to be taken of national rivalries, nor politics, race, religion, wealth or social status.

The first modern Games were held in Athens in 1896, and four years later, in Paris, women began to take part. Although the Winter Olympics did not begin until 1924, individual figure skating was part of the 1908 London Summer Olympics; both skating and ice hockey were successfully included in the Antwerp Games in 1920. But generally winter sports were felt to be too specialised. Only cold-weather countries had much experience of activities such as skiing – a means of transport overland across ice and snow during long winters.

The Scandinavians, for whom skiing is a part of everyday life, had objected to a Winter Games. They feared it would threaten their own Nordic Games, which had been held every four years since 1901. But the International Olympic Committee (IOC) agreed to stage an International Sports Week in Chamonix, France, in 1924. It was a success and the Scandinavians won 28 of the 43 medals, including nine golds. They dropped their objections and the event was retrospectively named the First Winter Olympic Games.

Apart from the Second World War period, the Winter Olympics were held every four years, a few months before the Summer Olympics. But in 1986 the IOC changed the schedule so that the Summer and Winter Games would be held in different years. Thus, for the only time in history, the Lillehammer (Norway) Games took place just two years after the previous Winter Olympics, which were held in Albertville, France.

Since the Winter Games began, 55 out of 56 gold medals in the men's Nordic skiing events have been won by competitors from Scandinavia or the former Soviet Union. For teams from warm weather countries, cross-country skiing can pose problems. At the Calgary Games in 1988, one competitor in the 50-kilometre event was so slow that race officials feared he was lost and sent out a search party. Roberto Alvarez of Mexico had never skied more than 20 kilometres before and finished 61st and last – 52 minutes behind the 60th place.

**Turn over ▶**

*Questions 28 – 32*

*Complete the table below.*

*Choose **ONE NUMBER ONLY** from the text for each answer.*

*Write your answers in boxes 28-32 on your answer sheet.*

| YEAR | EVENT |
|---|---|
| 28 ............. | Ancient Olympics came to an end |
| 29 ............ | First women's events |
| 30 ............ | First Nordic Games |
| 31 ............ | First winter team game included in Olympics |
| 32 ............ | First Winter Olympic Games |

*Questions 33 – 40*

*Do the following statements agree with the information given in the text?*

*In boxes 33-40 on your answer sheet, write*

| | |
|---|---|
| **TRUE** | *if the statement agrees with the information* |
| **FALSE** | *if the statement contradicts the information* |
| **NOT GIVEN** | *if there is no information on this* |

33 The spectators of the ancient Olympics, as well as the participants, were all male.

34 Only amateur athletes are allowed to compete in the modern Olympics.

35 The modern Olympics have always demonstrated the political neutrality intended by their founder.

36 The Antwerp Games proved that winter sports were too specialised.

37 One Winter Olympics has succeeded another every four years since 1924 with a break only for the Second World War.

38 The Albertville Winter Olympics took place in 1992.

39 Only Scandinavians have won gold medals in men's Winter Olympics Nordic skiing events.

40 Cross-country skiing events are a speciality of cold-weather countries.

Candidate Name _____

Candidate Number

INTERNATIONAL ENGLISH LANGUAGE TESTING SYSTEM **0380/2**

General Training Writing

**PRACTICE MATERIALS**     **Example 1**                    1 hour

Additional materials:
    Writing answer booklet

**Time**    1 hour

## INSTRUCTIONS TO CANDIDATES

Do not open this question paper until you are told to do so.

**Write your name and candidate number in the spaces at the top of this page.**

Read the instructions for each task carefully.

Answer both of the tasks.

Write at least 150 words for Task 1.

Write at least 250 words for Task 2.

Write your answers in the answer booklet.

Write clearly in pen or pencil. You may make alterations, but make sure your work is easy to read.

At the end of the test, hand in both this question paper and your answer booklet.

## INFORMATION FOR CANDIDATES

There are **two** tasks on this question paper.

Task 2 contributes twice as much as Task 1 to the Writing score.

   UNIVERSITY *of* CAMBRIDGE
ESOL Examinations

PV3
© UCLES 2009

## WRITING TASK 1

You should spend about 20 minutes on this task.

---

*There have been some problems with public transport in your area recently.*

*Write a letter to the manager of the public transport company.  In your letter*

- *describe the problems*
- *explain how these problems are affecting the public*
- *suggest what changes could be made*

---

Write at least 150 words.

You do **NOT** need to write any addresses.

Begin your letter as follows:

Dear Sir or Madam,

## WRITING TASK 2

You should spend about 40 minutes on this task.

Write about the following topic:

> ***Many people say that cooking and eating at home is better for the individual and the family than eating out in restaurants or canteens.***
>
> ***Do you agree or disagree?***

Give reasons for your answer and include any relevant examples from your own knowledge or experience.

Write at least 250 words.

Candidate Number

Candidate Name

## INTERNATIONAL ENGLISH LANGUAGE TESTING SYSTEM   **0380/2**

General Training Writing

**PRACTICE MATERIALS**    **Example 2**                               1 hour

Additional materials:
    Writing answer booklet

**Time**    1 hour

### INSTRUCTIONS TO CANDIDATES

Do not open this question paper until you are told to do so.

**Write your name and candidate number in the spaces at the top of this page.**

Read the instructions for each task carefully.

Answer both of the tasks.

Write at least 150 words for Task 1.

Write at least 250 words for Task 2.

Write your answers in the answer booklet.

Write clearly in pen or pencil. You may make alterations, but make sure your work is easy to read.

At the end of the test, hand in both this question paper and your answer booklet.

### INFORMATION FOR CANDIDATES

There are **two** tasks on this question paper.

Task 2 contributes twice as much as Task 1 to the Writing score.

PV3

© UCLES 2009

**WRITING TASK 1**

You should spend about 20 minutes on this task.

---

*You recently bought a large expensive item but when it was delivered to your home you found some problems with it.*

*Write a letter to the manager of the shop. In your letter*

- *give details of what you bought*
- *describe the problems with your item*
- *say what you want the shop to do*

---

Write at least 150 words.

You do **NOT** need to write any addresses.

Begin your letter as follows:

Dear Sir or Madam,

## WRITING TASK 2

You should spend about 40 minutes on this task.

Write about the following topic:

> **People should be allowed to continue to work for as long as they want to, and not be forced to retire at a particular age such as 60 or 65.**
>
> **Do you agree or disagree?**

Give reasons for your answer and include any relevant examples from your own knowledge or experience.

Write at least 250 words.

# The Speaking Test

Time: 11–14 minutes

Format: oral interview between examiner and candidate

Content: 3 parts

## Part 1 Introduction and interview
(4–5 minutes)

The examiner introduces him/herself and asks you to introduce yourself and confirm your identity.

The examiner asks you general questions on some familiar topics, e.g. home, family, work, studies, interests.

## Part 2 Individual long turn
(3–4 minutes, including 1 minute preparation time)

The examiner gives you a card which asks you to talk about a particular topic and which includes points that you can cover in your talk.

You are given one minute to prepare to talk about the topic on the card. You can make some notes to help you if you wish.

You talk for one to two minutes on the topic.

The examiner then asks you one or two questions on the same topic to finish this part of the test.

## Part 3 Two-way discussion
(4–5 minutes)

The examiner asks you further questions which are connected to the topic of Part 2.

These questions give you an opportunity to discuss more abstract issues and ideas.


All Speaking tests are recorded.

The practice materials on page 56 give you an example of the kinds of questions and tasks you could be asked to respond to in the Speaking test.

# Speaking Test Practice Materials

## Part 1

Let's talk about where you grew up.

- Describe the town or city where you grew up.
- Do you still live there now?
- Does your family still live there?
- Do you think the place has changed much since you were young?

## Part 2

*Candidate task card:*

**Describe a sports event you enjoyed watching.**

**You should say:**

> **what event you watched**
> **where you were**
> **who you watched it with**

**and explain why you enjoyed watching it.**

You will have to talk about the topic for 1 to 2 minutes.

You have 1 minute to think about what you are going to say.

You can make some notes to help you if you wish.

*Rounding-off questions:*

- Who won this event?
- Do you play this sport yourself?

## Part 3

Let's consider first of all watching sport …

- How expensive is it to go to sports events in your country?
- Do you think it's different watching a sports event on TV and going to watch it in person? In what ways?
- Do you think there's too much sport on TV? Why?

Finally, let's talk about famous sports people …

- Why do you think sports people often become media stars today?

# How to mark the Listening and Reading Practice Tests

Each question in the Listening and Reading tests is worth one mark.

## Questions which require letter/Roman numeral answers

- For questions where the answers are letters or Roman numerals, you should write *only* the number of answers required. For example, if the answer is a single letter or numeral you should write only one answer. If you write more letters or numerals than are required, your answer is *incorrect*.

## Questions which require answers in the form of words or numbers

- You may write your answers in upper or lower case.

- Words in brackets are *optional* – they are correct, but not necessary. If you write any other extra words that are not on the answer key, your answer is *incorrect*.

- Alternative answers are separated by a slash (/). If you write any of the alternative answers, your answer is *correct*.

- If you are asked to write an answer using a certain number of words and/or (a) number(s), you will be penalised if you exceed this. For example, if a question specifies an answer using NO MORE THAN THREE WORDS and the correct answer is 'black leather coat', the answer 'coat of black leather' is *incorrect*.

- In questions where you are expected to complete a gap, you should only copy the necessary missing word(s) or number(s) onto the answer sheet. For example, to complete 'in the … ', where the correct answer is 'morning', the answer 'in the morning' is *incorrect*.

- All answers require correct spelling, including any words in brackets. You should take care, therefore, when copying your answers onto the answer sheets.

- Both US and UK spelling are acceptable and are included in the answer key.

- All standard alternatives for numbers, dates and currencies are acceptable.

- All standard abbreviations are acceptable.

# Listening and Reading Practice Test Answer Keys

## Listening

### Section 1
| | |
|---|---|
| 1 | B |
| 2 | C |
| 3 | 15 minute |
| 4 | third/3rd year |
| 5 | first/1st Tuesday |
| 6 | 25% |
| 7 | room 12 |
| 8 | (Mrs) Waddell |
| 9 | window dressing / dress windows |
| 10 | black skirt |

### Section 2
| | |
|---|---|
| 11 | C |
| 12 | B |
| 13 | C |
| 14&15 | A |
| | D (in either order) |
| 16 | 75 |
| 17 | evening(s) |
| 18 | (4-course) dinner |
| 19 | 52 |
| 20 | golf club |

### Section 3
| | |
|---|---|
| 21 | weather (conditions) |
| 22 | Environment/Environmental Agency |
| 23 | B |
| 24 | A |
| 25 | C |
| 26 | B |
| 27 | B |
| 28 | C |
| 29 | A |
| 30 | A |

### Section 4
| | |
|---|---|
| 31 | Australia |
| 32 | (flight/flying) speed / speed of flight |
| 33 | looking/searching for food |
| 34 | start/begin to fly / start/begin flying |
| 35 | full/adult size / full adult size / full(y) grown |
| 36 | leave (the/their) nest(s) |
| 37 | die |
| 38 | attach (identification/ID/aluminium/ aluminum) rings |
| 39 | note (the) sex |
| 40 | (general) health |

## Academic Reading

### Section 1
| | |
|---|---|
| 1 | E |
| 2 | H |
| 3 | I |
| 4 | D |
| 5 | G |
| 6&7 | yeast |
| | bacteria (in either order) |
| 8 | protein |
| 9 | chemical solvents |
| 10 | (small) holes |
| 11 | FALSE |
| 12 | TRUE |
| 13 | NOT GIVEN |

### Section 2
| | |
|---|---|
| 14 | A |
| 15 | D |
| 16 | B |
| 17 | C |
| 18 | C |
| 19 | D |
| 20 | C |
| 21 | B |
| 22 | Egypt |
| 23 | monks |
| 24 | Ptolemy |
| 25 | (navigation) satellites |
| 26 | (some) cars |

### Section 3
| | |
|---|---|
| 27 | iv |
| 28 | vii |
| 29 | v |
| 30 | i |
| 31 | iii |
| 32 | B |
| 33 | B |
| 34 | D |
| 35 | A |
| 36 | D |
| 37 | FALSE |
| 38 | NOT GIVEN |
| 39 | TRUE |
| 40 | FALSE |

## General Training Reading

### Section 1
| | |
|---|---|
| 1 | A |
| 2 | E |
| 3 | A (and) F (in either order; both required for 1 mark) |
| 4 | B (and) E (in either order; both required for 1 mark) |
| 5 | 166 |
| 6 | 010 |
| 7 | 130 |
| 8 | 101 |
| 9 | 170 |
| 10 | 101 |
| 11 | (staircase) J |
| 12 | (in) (the) courtyard |
| 13 | evacuate ((the) building) |
| 14 | (the) Reception |

### Section 2
| | |
|---|---|
| 15 | iii |
| 16 | x |
| 17 | v |
| 18 | vi |
| 19 | viii |
| 20 | ii |
| 21 | iv |
| 22 | (registered) medical practitioner |
| 23 | basic salary |
| 24 | length of service |
| 25 | 15 weeks |
| 26 | (a) pregnancy-related illness |
| 27 | (annual) leave |

### Section 3
| | |
|---|---|
| 28 | 393 |
| 29 | 1900 |
| 30 | 1901 |
| 31 | 1920 |
| 32 | 1924 |
| 33 | TRUE |
| 34 | NOT GIVEN |
| 35 | NOT GIVEN |
| 36 | FALSE |
| 37 | FALSE |
| 38 | TRUE |
| 39 | FALSE |
| 40 | TRUE |

# Listening Tapescript

## SECTION 1

**You will hear the manager of a shop talking to a new employee called Penny.**

(*Knocking*)

M: Come in. Good morning. It's …

P: Penny Marne.

M: Ah yes … Penny. Do sit down. Now I know a lot of things emerged during your interview last week, but I thought it was worth going over the essential stuff again.

P: Yes, absolutely. That'll be very helpful.

M: The first thing is that given your interest in fashions we've decided to put you in the Dress Department.

P: Oh that's great. Is that next to the children's section?

M: Yes. Now we've given the section a new name actually. From next week it's going to be called the Young Set.

P: Youngster?

M: No. Two words – the Young Set.

P: Right, sorry.

M: Now, you'll be required to work a five and a half day week. We're closed on Wednesday afternoon and Sunday, of course.

P: Do we get overtime for Saturday?

M: Well, actually, we used to give an extra $2 an hour, but then we decided to make it a flat rate of $6.50 an hour.

P: OK fine. And the actual hours?

M: 9 – 5 with an hour for lunch and 15 minute coffee breaks.

P: And what about holidays?

M: Well, it's three weeks in the first year and that rises to four weeks in your third year with us. Now we do give you on-the-job training which we conduct during normal hours, so you'll be paid for that.

P: Which day?

M: It's on the first Tuesday of every month.

M: Now, in addition to your basic pay I should explain that you're entitled to some staff perks which our assistants do find a valuable benefit.

P: Do we get a discount?

M: That's right – 25% off everything in the store, although we do make an exception for sale goods, which I'm afraid have no discount.

P: Yeah, fine. And I was wondering about pension arrangements?

M: You get a good company pension, which our Personnel Manager will be able to explain to you in detail. She's in

Room 12 – worth going along to see her.

P: And who will I be working under – Mr Appleby?

M: The manager of your section is Mrs Waddell. That's W-A-D-D-E-double L …

P: Mrs Waddell. OK, and apart from serving the customers, will I have any other duties?

M: Good question. We do ask you to do the window dressing.

P: Oh, I'll enjoy that.

M: And one of the biggest worries in the boutique is shoplifters, so you have to check for them.

P: Will I receive training on that?

M: Yes, certainly. That'll be one of the sessions next month. Oh, and we'll be asking you to check stock.

P: Right … yes, course. And is there a particular dress code in the shop?

M: Right … well, we're quite flexible, but what we'd do is ask you to wear a black skirt and the shop will give you a red blouse. We'll also give you a name badge which you must wear all the time.

P: Yeah, of course.

M: Right. Is there anything else you'd like to ask me?

P: No, that's very comprehensive. Thank you.

M: Good. So we'll see you on Monday.

P: Yes, thank you. Goodbye.

M: Goodbye.

## SECTION 2

**You will hear a recorded message giving information about an English hotel.**

Welcome to the Bridge Hotel Information Line. The Bridge Hotel is part of the Compact Group, which is a large association of family-owned hotels offering a warm friendly atmosphere and high quality service at competitive prices. All of them cater for a wide range of people – from business to leisure clients.

Set in a quiet residential area on the attractive outskirts of Belford, about three miles from the city centre, the Bridge Hotel is a popular choice for conferences. After recent refurbishment and expansion, it now has 25 double rooms and 20 singles. All 45 are en suite with TV and coffee- and tea-making facilities.

The Bridge Hotel is set in three and a half hectares of grounds with an open-air swimming pool and four tennis courts. There is also a newly opened gym with fitness suite, which is considered one of the best equipped in the area. Non-resident membership is available.

We have a fully licensed restaurant for residents and non-residents, which provides a wide range of dishes with a particular focus on dishes from around the world.

For the discerning business customer, we have designated business rooms with phone links allowing full internet access. Our conference facilities cater for up to 200 delegates and we are able to offer transport to guests to and from Birmingham Airport at a small extra cost.

There now follows information about short break packages.

Welcome to the Bridge Hotel Short Breaks Information Line. We offer three packages: 2-day, 3-day and 5-day.

The 2-day costs £75 per person per night and includes full cooked breakfast and evening entertainment. Very popular for weekend getaways.

The 3-day break costs £60 per person per night and in addition to offers for the 2-day break, includes one 4-course dinner. This allows guests to enjoy the full range of hotel facilities.

The 5-day break costs £52 per person per night and, in addition to offers from the 2- and 3-day breaks, includes free beauty therapy on two days and a full-day pass to a golf club. This package is particularly popular with couples who want a completely relaxing break.

If you would like more information about these special packages, call extension 3469 to speak to our Customer Service Manager, John Martin.

Thank you for calling the Bridge Hotel Information Line.

## SECTION 3

**You will hear two students called Katy and Harry, discussing a project they are both working on.**

K:   Hi, Harry.

H:   Katy, hi. Look, let's sit down and work out what we've got to do for this next project we've got for the geography course. I'm glad we're doing it together. We should be able to split it between us so it's not too much work!

K:   Yes, Harry – I had quite a long chat about it with Dr Smith yesterday, so I've got quite a good idea of how we should be organising it. Now, he said we've got to move on from the general project we did on soil erosion and look specifically at coastal change. I think that'll be interesting, don't you?

H:   Yeah. I was thinking about it last night because we'll have to make sure we pick our days to visit the beaches. It seems there's a reasonable train service to White Sands Bay but the weather could stop us from getting all the samples we need. It could take us longer than we think.

K:   Hmmm – yeah, but we could save ourselves some time if we try to get hold of any information that's already been collected. I know several post-graduates who have done stuff in White Sands Bay this year, though on other topics.

We could check out what the Marine Biology Unit have got – they're bound to have something we could use.

H:   OK – let's do that this week and arrange to go to the beach next week. I think we'll need about three days. If we book ahead, we can probably stay in the University lodge when we're down there. The other thing is, we must go to the Environment Agency and get permission to take the samples, just in case anyone challenges us when we're down there. I think we'll have to fill out a form or something.

K:   Right, Harry, now let's work out who's going to do what first, because we have to get it done by the end of this month. I think we ought to divide up the data collection between us.

H:   What? So only one of us goes to the beach, do you mean?

K:   No, I think we both ought to get a picture of what's involved, but there's no need for us both to do everything. I mean, when we're at the beach you could go to both ends and make sure we have the set of shots we need to illustrate where erosion has taken place.

H:   OK, fine.

K:   And I'll move up the beach and pick up the different stones and put sand in bags. Does that seem fair to you?

H:   Yeah, OK. Then what about the other stuff? Do you want me to go and do the questionnaires while you're on the beach? We'll get more people that way. Or is it better if we do them together?

K:   I think that would be better. We could set aside a whole day for it.

H:   What about the lab work – looking at what we've collected and testing it?

K:   I don't mind doing it, but I'm pretty slow.

H:   OK. You can leave that to me.

K:   Fine.

H:   Then that leaves us two weeks to write it up ready for the presentation to the class on the 29th. Shall we do the presentation together? Like you do the first bit and me the second? Actually, no – I think that can be a bit muddling for the class. I'd like to do the presentation, if you don't mind.

K:   Fine by me.

H:   It's just that it won't affect the marks that *you* get – I mean it's not like I get more for actually doing it – the tutor will judge it as a whole. But I think I remember them saying at the beginning of the year that we were expected to do three before the end of the year in order to get a satisfactory mark, and I'm one behind, whereas you've already done yours, haven't you? I can see why they put them into the course, because most interviews for jobs demand you do a presentation nowadays.

K:   Yeah. Does that mean I have to write it up? I think it'll be impossible to do that together.

H:   Yes. You're very good at that.

K:   Oh yes! Typical that I get landed with it as usual. Actually, I don't mind. I know we haven't got very long but that's OK. Often I write better when I'm pushed for time – it focuses the mind! But I'll have to have a think about how we present the data, because that won't be straightforward like the rest, so I'd like a bit of help with that …

H:   Yeah, sure. Anyway, I was thinking – after we've done the presentation I think it'd be a good idea if we asked our classmates to tell us what they think of our conclusions.

K:   Well, I dunno. They won't have done the research, so whatever they say would be uninformed.

H:   I don't agree. I mean, they've all worked on something similar, so they know what's involved and it would be useful to see how they think ours stands up. We'll have to be sure of our ground – make sure we don't make any mistakes in our results or whatever. I don't mean I think they're going to tell us anything new – just give us their thoughts on the process.

K:   OK. Then I'll deal with the questions at the end. Dr Smith said we would have to prepare thoroughly for this and I'll probably get lots of background stuff in the process of writing up, so I'll be prepared for any surprises! If he's impressed by your presentation then we should do well.

H:   Right.

## SECTION 4

**You will hear a talk by a university lecturer in Australia on a type of bird called a peregrine falcon.**

I'm Professor Sam Richards, and I've come as the third guest lecturer on this course in Australian birds of prey. My job is to keep a watchful scientific eye on the state of Tasmanian peregrines, so I'll start by giving you some background to these magnificent birds of prey before I speak briefly on my own project.

Peregrine falcons are found on all continents with the exception of Antarctica. So don't go looking for them at the South Pole. They are found almost everywhere in Australia and it's interesting to note that the name, peregrine, implies that they are wanderers – that they move from place to place following the seasons – and indeed, in most parts of the world they are migratory birds. But not in Australia, however, where they prefer to stay in one place.

They are known to be the world's fastest creature and they have been tracked by radar diving down towards the ground at 180 km an hour. However, a number of textbooks claim that their flight speed can go as high as 350 km an hour, so there is still some dispute about just how fast they can actually fly.

Female peregrine falcons, like all other Australian falcons, are larger than their male counterparts; in fact the female is almost a third larger than the male in the case of peregrines. While she stays close to the nest to protect the eggs and the young chicks, the male is mostly occupied looking for food.

Peregrines typically lay two or three eggs per nest and, after the eggs have hatched, when the chicks are about 20 days old, they start to fly. So they fly at a very young age. By the time they are just 28 days old, they have already reached full adult size; in other words, they are fully grown. Soon after this, at about two months after hatching from the egg, they leave the nest for good. From this point on they're on their own. Unlike their parents, which have learned how to hunt, the young falcons are not good at feeding themselves and so during the first year about 60% of them die. Once the birds have managed to live to breeding age, at two years old, they generally go on to live for another six or seven years.

When we come across nests with young chicks, the first thing we do is catch the chicks before they are able to fly. We have to catch them at an early age. We then attach identification rings to their legs. These rings are made of colour-coded aluminium and they allow us to identify the birds through binoculars later in their lives. Thirdly, because we need to know how many males and how many female chicks are being born, we note the sex of the chicks. Noting the sex of the birds is a vital part of our research, as I will discuss later. The next thing to do is to take a blood sample from the chicks. We take the blood sample so that we can check the level of pesticide in their bodies. Peregrine falcons can build dangerous quantities of pesticides in their blood stream by feeding on smaller mammals which in turn feed on crops, grown on farms where pesticides are used. Finally we check the birds thoroughly, really checking the birds for their general health. This whole process only takes a few minutes; in fact, most of our time in the field is actually spent trying to find the nests, not on the data collection itself.

Well, that's all I have for you today. If you'd like to do some further reading …

# Interpreting your Scores

## Your score in Listening

### Scores 26 and above

If you have strictly followed the guidelines on page 3, you are likely to get an acceptable score on the IELTS Listening test under examination conditions, but remember that different institutions will find different scores acceptable.

### Scores 15–25

You may not get an acceptable score on the IELTS Listening test under examination conditions and we recommend that you think about having more lessons or practice before you take IELTS.

### Scores 0–14

You are highly unlikely to get an acceptable score on the IELTS Listening test under examination conditions and we recommend that you spend a lot of time improving your English before you take IELTS.

## Your score in Academic Reading

### Scores 26 and above

If you have strictly followed the guidelines on page 3, you are likely to get an acceptable score on the IELTS Academic Reading test under examination conditions, but remember that different institutions will find different scores acceptable.

### Scores 14–25

You may not get an acceptable score on the IELTS Academic Reading test under examination conditions and we recommend that you think about having more lessons or practice before you take IELTS.

### Scores 0–13

You are highly unlikely to get an acceptable score on the IELTS Academic Reading test under examination conditions and we recommend that you spend a lot of time improving your English before you take IELTS.

## Your score in General Training Reading

### Scores 28 and above

If you have strictly followed the guidelines on page 3, you are likely to get an acceptable score on the IELTS General Training Reading test under examination conditions, but remember that different institutions will find different scores acceptable.

### Scores 17–27

You may not get an acceptable score on the IELTS General Training Reading test under examination conditions and we recommend that you think about having more lessons or practice before you take IELTS.

### Scores 0–16

You are highly unlikely to get an acceptable score on the IELTS General Training Reading test under examination conditions and we recommend that you spend a lot of time improving your English before you take IELTS.

Please note the following:

- The above recommendations are based on the average scores which the majority of institutions and organisations accept. However, different institutions and organisations accept different scores for different purposes. The institution to which you are applying may require a higher or lower score than most other institutions. Please check score requirements for individual institutions on the IELTS website **www.ielts.org**

- Your performance in the real IELTS test will be reported in two ways: there will be a Band Score from 1 to 9 for each of the skills; and an Overall Band Score from 1 to 9. Both the Band Scores for each skill and the Overall Band Score may be reported in whole or half bands. The Overall Band Score is the average of your scores in the four skills. For example, if you score Band 6 for Listening, Band 6 for Reading, Band 5 for Writing and Band 7 for Speaking, your Overall Band Score will be:

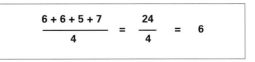

$$\frac{6+6+5+7}{4} = \frac{24}{4} = 6$$

You will see from this example that a lower score in one skill can be compensated for by higher scores in the others.

- Institutions or organisations considering your application are advised to look at both the Overall Band Score and the Band Scores for each skill to make sure you have the language skills needed for a particular purpose. For example, if your course has a lot of reading and writing, but no lectures, listening comprehension might not be very important and a score of, say, 5 in Listening might be acceptable if the Overall Band Score was 7. However, for a course where there are lots of lectures and spoken instructions, a score of 5 in Listening might be unacceptable even though the Overall Band Score was 7.

- This Practice Test has been checked so that it is approximately the same level of difficulty as the real IELTS test. However, we cannot guarantee that your score in the Practice Test will be reflected in the real IELTS test. The Practice Test can only give you an idea of your possible future performance and it is up to you to decide whether you are ready to take IELTS.

# How Writing is Assessed

The Academic and General Training Writing tests both consist of two tasks, Task 1 and Task 2. Each task is assessed independently.

Writing performance is assessed by certified examiners who are appointed by the test centre and approved by the British Council or IDP: IELTS Australia.

The examiner rates the candidate's responses using detailed performance descriptors which describe writing performance at the nine IELTS bands. These descriptors apply to both the Academic and General Training Writing tests.

**Task 1** responses are assessed on the following four criteria:

*Task Achievement*
This criterion refers to how appropriately, accurately and relevantly the response fulfils the requirements of the task. Responses must be at least 150 words in length.

Academic Writing Task 1 is an information-transfer task with a defined response which requires candidates to draw on the factual content of a diagram. Candidates are not expected to speculate or explain any areas that lie outside the input material.

General Training Writing Task 1 is also a task with a defined response which requires candidates to write a letter in response to an everyday situation or problem. The input material describes the context and purpose of the letter and the functions candidates should cover in their responses.

*Coherence and Cohesion*
This criterion refers to the overall clarity and fluency of the message: how the response organises and links information, ideas and language. Coherence refers to the linking of ideas through logical sequencing. Cohesion refers to the varied and appropriate use of cohesive devices (for example, logical connectors, pronouns and conjunctions) to assist in making the references and relationships between and within sentences clear.

*Lexical Resource*
This criterion refers to the range of vocabulary the candidate uses and the accuracy and appropriacy of that use.

*Grammatical Range and Accuracy*
This criterion refers to the range and accurate use of the candidate's grammatical resource at sentence level.

**Task 2** responses are assessed on the following four criteria:

*Task Response*
This criterion refers to the candidate's ability to formulate and develop a position in relation to a question or statement. Ideas should be supported by evidence, and examples may be drawn from the candidate's own experience. Responses must be at least 250 words in length.

*Coherence and Cohesion*
As for Task 1.

*Lexical Resource*
As for Task 1.

*Grammatical Range and Accuracy*
As for Task 1.

All criteria have equal weighting.

Task 2 contributes twice as much as Task 1 to the Writing score.

Candidates should note that they will lose marks in Writing if their responses are a) under the minimum word length, b) partly or wholly plagiarised, c) not written as full, connected text (e.g. if the response is in note form, if bullet points are used etc).

The public version of the Writing band descriptors is available on the IELTS website **www.ielts.org**

# Sample Candidate Writing Responses and Examiner Comments

On the following pages, you will find candidate responses to the five Writing Practice Tests. There is one response for each Writing task. Below each response, you will find examiner comments and the Band Scores given.

The examiner guidelines for assessing candidate performance on the Writing test are very detailed. There are many different ways a candidate may achieve a particular Band Score. The candidate responses that follow should not be regarded as definitive examples of any particular Band Score.

## Academic Writing Example 1 – Task 1

### Sample Response 1

The Japanese Tourists started travelling to Australia in 1985 were around 4.5 millions and in the following year it had gone up 1/4 million more than 1985. The number of tourist increased steadily till 1990 from 1/2 million to 1 1/2 million and at the same time it there was, fell in the figure in 1991 about 1/4 million tourists comparing the 1990 as one can say it surges. In 1992 it picked up again and gone upto 1 1/4 million tourist (ie) 3/4 million more than the year 1991. In 1993 it reached up 12 million tourists and in 1994 and gone steadily increased till 1995. In 1994 it reached 13 3/4 million and in 1995 it touched around 15 1/2 million tourists.

In the same time if you talk in percentage of the Japanese tourist between 1985 to 1995 (ie) Australia's share of Japan's tourist Market it stared from a percentage to 6 percentage in 1995 and at the same time it reached its peak in 1994 more than 6.25%. When you see the graph it gone upto 4.9% in 1989 and there was a surge again in 1990, and it was about 4.25%. The increased started from 1991 till 1994 at the rate of 2% approximately every year and at last in 1995 the percentage dropped about .25%.

The highest Japanese tourists travelling abroad was in 1995 and at the same time highest percentage was 1994 (ie) 6.25%

### Examiner Comments

**Band 5**

This answer includes the main points of the information but these are inaccurately reported and hard to identify because so much detail is given. The figures are confused and sometimes inaccurate. The candidate has tried to organise the information logically, but linking is repetitive and not always clear. The range of vocabulary is enough to describe the information, and spelling is quite well controlled. The writer tries to use a wider range at times but makes errors in word choice and word formation. Similarly, the writer tries to use some complex sentences, but errors in grammar, especially in verb phrases, are common and make the writing difficult to understand in places. This is a good example of a Band 5 response.

# Academic Writing Example 1 – Task 2

## Sample Response 2

There are many kinds of work people interested in at companies. Young people are not enough work experience in their lives so they consider to try to work in a shop.

Most people need to work experience in their lives before they apply to the many kinds of companies. They interested in work in their lives and have experience because they want to know how to do work in a area of position in their lives.

People enjoy their work experience. When young people are learn to how to work that have good experience because they can understand their parents of work for the stricts. However if they do not have work experience they do not understand what do they feel therefore it is important to them.

Many people have confidence and responsibility. When they have work experience. They need to have confidence about their work because. If they do not have their confidence their job is not succeed so they need to have confidence. Also they need to have responsibility because if they do not have responsibility they have trouble with customer therefore that company is not reliable from customer. Also consumer have give to claim to the company so the company have problem. However when young people learn to those things it is good for them.

Many countries children do not know how to strict area about work place. They usually go to school and studying so they do not know how to strict place therefore if they have work experience they can learn and think about work.

## Examiner Comments

### Band 3.5

This answer is obviously related to the topic, but there is no clear response to any part of the question and it is difficult to identify any relevant point of view. There is some attempt to use paragraphs and basic connectives, but there is little logical progression. Instead the ideas are very repetitive and circular both within and between paragraphs. The range of vocabulary is limited and so there is frequent repetition of basic vocabulary and words taken from the question. There are occasional examples of a wider range but there are also errors in word choice and spelling that confuse the reader. The candidate attempts to use a range of structures, but the lack of control of grammar and punctuation results in strain for the reader. Although the writing has some features of Band 4 performance, no part of the question is successfully addressed and this limits the rating to Band 3.5.

## Academic Writing Example 2 – Task 1

**Sample Response 3**

> The diagram illustrates how to use water in order to generate electricity.
>
> The diagram shows that the process of producing electricity involves as natural resouces, like water, as well as special human-built equipment.
> First of all, the sun energy evaporates some of the water from a sea. Evaporation ~~forces~~ forces Clouds to form. While the rain goes
>
> the water is collected in a purpose built reservoir.
> Afterwards, from a dam the water goes through a valve. This movement force a turbine to rotate and this process generates electricity.
> Finally, the electricity is transferred by high voltage cables to a transformer station. The transformer station ~~supply~~ supplies city buildings such as schools and hospitals with electricity.
> Moreover, the diagram indicates that the water which is ~~used~~ involved in ~~of~~ the process is used repeatedly. From the toerbin it goes to a pump and than returnes to the reservoir.
> Overall, the illustration shows that ~~there are the electricity~~ 3 main ~~ep~~ steps in order to generate electricity: collecting the water, ~~producing cedectricity and~~ rotating the tourbin and accumulating ~~ea~~ electricity in the transformer station.

## Examiner Comments

### Band 7

This answer includes a clear overview of the process and the information is well-selected with good coverage of the key points. Some of the points could however be further extended. The candidate has organised the information logically with a clear progression of information through the answer. Some good linkers are used although there are occasional mistakes in their use. The writer has made efforts to adapt the vocabulary in the task but there are spelling mistakes with some words. There are a number of complex grammatical structures which are used accurately and although there are some errors in word order and the use of articles, these do not reduce the clarity of the writing.

## Academic Writing Example 2 – Task 2

**Sample Response 4**

Old buildings not only are still useful, but also keep the history alive. Not all of them have enough history to say that it's better to maintain it. In my opinion only the buildings that really involve nation's history could be maintain, because it will remain to the people the traditions, culture, and stories that relevant people lived before, and this is part of the formal education of each person.

Most of the countries of the world at least have important people that help to constructed the nation, or fight for the independence, or are just important because They changed the social, political, economical or even musical environment of their countries. When people see the places where this people lived and where they develop their arts, these places or buildings help to reconstruct the stories and are useful for imagine how was the situation before. So every time that people will see this buildings or monuments they are able to remain the history and also learn about it. Finally nowadays human beings are capable to maintain this buildings in good conditions, even they can modernise them but without change their principal structure and fonds.

On the other hand it's true that the cities of the world have to continue with its development. Therefore they have to build new buildings that allow people work with better and modern environments that let them work efficiently, and also that offer development resources. New buildings brings new technologie as well, that could improve the efficience, productivity and production of different companies, organizations, shops, offices, etc.

In conclusion some buildings would be knocked down to make way progress and development. However that old buildings that have important history for human beings should be maintains. If we knocked down these buildings we would knocked down our traditions, culture, history and even some part of our lives.

**Examiner Comments**

**Band 6**

The answer addresses both questions in the task, but the second question is only treated in a general way and so this aspect is not sufficiently developed. Nevertheless there is a clear argument that progresses logically in spite of some repetition. Connectives are used but linking between sentences is sometimes omitted, while referencing is not always clear. The range of language is adequate for the task, and there are examples of some less common words, which are used appropriately. The candidate makes mistakes in word form and spelling, but the meaning is still clear. There is a range of structures, though complex structures are not always successful and errors in grammar and tense are noticeable. However, these do not usually cause problems for the reader. Overall this is a clear example of a Band 6 response.

# Academic Writing Example 3 – Task 1

## Sample Response 5

When we see the graph, domestic household is different of others. According to the graph number of complaints remained stable about factories noise from 1984 to 1966. It means most of skills and something are made from factories. However society is getting change, so in the future people don't have to go factories, they can do most of things' at home. Maybe factories will be decrease. Number of complaints dropped steadly about road works from 1980 to 1996. It shows us most of road works, were formed in the past. Now days people don't have to road works because there already were todays. Number of complaints increased sharply about traffic noise from 1990 to 1996. It remained the same from 1980 to 1984 then it dropped from 1985 to 1988. However it increased from 1988, it means many people have their own car and society is getting change. Now-days cars are neccessary in our life and it will be increase continues.

Number of complaints reached almost peak about domestic household in 1996. It increased suddenly from 1990, and it is highest to others. It means people want domestic and many people did that.

## Examiner Comments

### Band 4

There is no introduction to the topic in this answer, so the opening is rather confusing. The candidate has tried to describe the key information but gives no figures and the focus is lost in the irrelevant explanations and excessive detail. The information is not well selected or logically organised, so it is difficult to follow the message. New points are not linked into the summary and relationships between points are not clearly signalled, although some basic linking words are used. The range of vocabulary is limited and even though the writer tries to use a range of structures, there is a lack of grammatical control and frequent errors in quite basic structures. This is a good example of a Band 4 response.

# Academic Writing Example 3 – Task 2

## Sample Response 6

the evolution in technology nowadays is very rampant. People do not even recognize changes from one to another. there are a lot of modern equipment, appliances and even simple machines are available in the market. Competitors in business industries keep doing transformation, product deve-lopment and more research work. Sometimes their own products compete each other. One of these modern equipments or appliances in the market that is very salable is the television.

Television dominates the communication and entertainment industries long time ago. Starting from the Black and White TV, here comes the Colored TV. In addition, Cable TV is now available in the market. In Southeast Asia, particularly in the Philippines, the most salable appliances in the market is the television. Even the ordinary vendors in the market or in the side walk avail one so that they can watch television while working. Business men and employees watch TV for news and general information. House keepers and house-wives, together with the children entertain themselves with the variety shows and soap operas through television. Everyone, in all walks of life uses television as one of their 'mate' in life there are Some issues that modernization, new technology including television is dangerous for children & for the whole family because it destroys a sense of community and belongingness and sometimes it influence the young people in their principle in life.

In conclusion, television is a modern appliance that can help a lot in the life of each and everyone. It has its' own disadvantages too. It can do good or can influence bad paradigms to the people, but I believe that the result of the use or watching TV depends on the person or family themselves. Together w/ the development is the consequence of having great discipline in oneself.

## Examiner Comments

### Band 5

This answer does not focus sufficiently on the question and a lot of irrelevant material is included. It is difficult to identify the candidate's position on the topic or to extract the main ideas. There is some organisation, but the development of the answer is not wholly logical. A range of linking words is used, but these are sometimes inaccurate and in some sections the candidate does not clearly signal how ideas relate to each other. There is a clear attempt to use an ambitious range of vocabulary, but there are a lot of inappropriate choices that indicate limited control. Similarly, the writer uses a mix of complex and simple sentences but makes fairly basic errors. Although there are some features of higher level performance in this script, the lack of focus and clear development limit the overall rating to Band 5.

# General Training Writing Example 1 – Task 1

## Sample Response 7

Dear Sir or Madam,

Hi. I write you this letter to report some problems which public transport in my area recently.

I live in Blair Athol and usually take Bus 224 from my home to Mawson Lakes Campus. But in the last 4 weeks, the bus has been frequently late. Sometimes the bus arrived late up to 20 minutes. The timetable seems useless. As a result, I have been caught late for the courses several times, which is embarrassing. I don't know what the reason is for the problem, but it's obviously affecting people's regular lives. For instance,

if a stuff comes to work late, he may lose his customers, and even worse, he may lose his job. People may endure a few times of the late transport, but they cannot hold on for many times. People need precise and accurate arrangement with their lives.

So, I suggest you could solve this problem as soon as possible. Please notify the drivers to be on time. If current timetable is outdated, please notify the public the change. I wish this can be solved after you receive my letter.

Thanks for your attention.

Regards

Yours

## Examiner Comments

### Band 6.5

This letter has a clear purpose and all the content is relevant. The bullet points are well-covered but could be more fully extended. Apart from the overly informal opening and closing, the tone of the letter is consistently appropriate. The organisation of the letter is logical and there is very good use throughout of linking devices. The vocabulary resource is large enough to allow for some flexible and precise use, although there are some inappropriacies and occasional spelling errors. Errors in word order are noticeable, as is omission of prepositions and articles, but complex sentences including relative clauses and conditionals are accurate.

**Sample Response 8**

Everyone has to eat. The question is, where to eat? You may cook and eat at home, or just eat out in restaurants or canteens. My personal opinion is that eating at home is better for the individual and the family than eating out.

First, it has no doubt that cooking and eating at home can save a lot of money. Generally, the cost of eating in restaurants is much higher than eating at home. By cooking at home, you don't have to pay the labor fee for the chef, and don't have to pay tips to the waiter. What you have to do is just a little hand operation and a little time. From supermarkets, you can buy cheap vegetables and meat, which may cost only 10 percent of the same food in a restaurant. Sometimes, you can get cheaper food in discount time. Especially, a big family may enjoy the method, as the monthly cost would be less.

Second, you can freely select your favorite food to cook. A restaurant cannot always provide you with delicious food. The taste of food in restaurants is usually designed for the public, which is not suitable for a particular guest. If you miss the taste of your mum's soup, it's not likely to find the same one in a restaurant. In this case, the best choice is to cook by yourself, to reproduce your mum's food to the best you can.

Finally, it's obvious that eating at home is more healthy and clean. You don't know whether it's dirty in the restaurants, and also you don't know whether the food is fresh. But by cooking at home, you can know everything about the cooking materials. Moreover, it's easy to control the usage of fat and oil, unless you don't care to become too fat.

In brief, I believe that eating at home is healthy and clean. If people want to save money, eating at home is also a good choice. In addition, people can cook what they like as well. So I personally prefer eating at home.

## Examiner Comments

### Band 7

This writer states a clear position at the outset and maintains it to the end, where all the arguments are summed up and the position re-stated. The answer progresses clearly to its conclusion, with some good use of cohesive devices. Paragraphing is also well-handled and helps the reader. The ideas are logically organised and each main idea is supported with additional information. There are some errors in referencing. The range of vocabulary includes some original and less frequent items specific to the task. There are some inappropriate word choices, but the meaning is still clear. Spelling errors are rare, and there is a good variety of sentence structures.

# General Training Writing Example 2 – Task 1

## Sample Response 9

Dear Sir or Madam

I feel I must express my disappointment

I have received a new air conditioning system which has heating system as well. It is a new design in this year, convenient button function, and can fix on the wall. When I received, I was absolutely delighted. However I was using for 3 nights. Unfortunately I found some problems with it. Firstly If I switch it on it was such a big noisy. Secondly, as we all know nowadays very cold. Thus I bought this incredibly heating system doesn't working. If I turn on the heating switch only blew the cold wind.

Consequently I couldn't sleep over very well.

In addition, I had ordered marvelous violet colour. However I received fair beige colour. it was quite unbalance with my furnitures. I am still very upsetting. I think that is not reasonable cost. I paid over £2000.

I think you would consider to give me discount it if I go to your shop again. And changing the another air conditiong system and heating system which is violet colour as soon as possible.

I look forward to hearing from you shortly

Yours faithfully

## Examiner Comments

### Band 5.5

This answer generally provides all the information required by the task, but the purpose seems incomplete without reference to the shop at the start of the letter. There is no reference to this being an item bought at the shop, even though it is evident that the writer is complaining. The answer is organised and there is a clear progression in the letter. The writing contains a range of connectives and some of these are used effectively to relate ideas. In some sections, however, these cohesive devices are used mechanically at the start of almost every sentence. The range of vocabulary is sufficient for the task and is a strong feature of the answer, in spite of some inappropriate word choice and some errors in word form. There is also a range of structures, with a mix of simple and complex sentences. However, control of syntax, basic grammar and punctuation is weak at times and errors are quite frequent. The flaws in setting out the purpose of the letter and the frequent grammatical errors limit this script to Band 5.5.

**Sample Response 10**

In this task two, I want to like the people should be allowed to continue to work for as long as they want to. If the people are working in some concern, or the Government, they are always very free in mind, and they can "earn more money". If one can earn lot, he spend it some thing. Like most of the people want to build a house first, then they get many facilities. All are wanted now-a-days earn more money and they buy a car, all well furnished house, furniture, good articles, (espically ladies spend lot of the money in her valuable articles, such as gold chain, neclace, bangles, and earings etc..;]

In this context, I want to clarify one thing. That is if the Government or such concern are to restrict once "retirement", All of a sudden people will depressed

In my opinion, one who is elegible for working in his line, the company or the Government will not "disturbed", or forced to retire the people.

The concern can give all the facilities to their employees, like, House Rent, conveyance allowance, educational allowance and the most important thing is the medical facilities are provide for their employers. one who satisfied in his or her job, they can wonderfully worked for (his or her) concern. So the Government or any other companies are always give much more importants to the employers.

In my opinion again I will tell the companies & Governments "do not forced to retire at a particular age such as 60 or 65". In a person who is not able to work in his 50th year, then he applied voluntary retirement. In this aspect the concern to must provide all the benefit to this person. Such as, provident fund, ESI, merical allowance and retirement-benefits.

One who is satisfied his job, his life is automatically pleasent and his mind is peacefull. So the major companies are give more and more facilities.

Finally, I would like to request all the concerns, do not forced to ritire at a patticular age limit in his employers. Please allowed people should enjoy and continue to work for as long as they want. This is in my view point, to tell the good companies and all the Governments.

Thanking you.

## Examiner Comments

### Band 4.5

The answer focuses on the question, but is quite repetitive. Ideas are not well developed and lack clarity, and some supporting ideas seem to be irrelevant. It is difficult to follow the argument or to understand how ideas relate to each other. Linking expressions and paragraphing are used, but not appropriately, and this creates problems for the reader. The range of vocabulary is the best feature of this answer as it is sufficient for a discussion of the topic, in spite of repetition of some inappropriate word choices. The control of grammar and sentence structures is weak, however, and the number of errors makes it difficult for the reader to extract the meaning at times. The range of vocabulary raises this script to Band 4.5.

# How Speaking is Assessed

The Speaking test assesses whether candidates can communicate effectively in English.

Speaking performance is assessed by certificated examiners who are appointed by the test centre and approved by the British Council or IDP: IELTS Australia.

The examiner rates the candidate's performance throughout the Speaking test, using detailed performance descriptors. These describe speaking performance at the nine IELTS bands according to four different criteria:

*Fluency and Coherence*
This criterion refers to the ability to talk with normal levels of continuity, rate and effort, and to link ideas and language together to form coherent, connected speech.

Speech rate and speech continuity provide evidence of the fluency criterion.

Logical sequencing of spoken sentences, clear marking of stages in a discussion, narration or argument, and the use of cohesive devices (e.g. connectors, pronouns and conjunctions) within and between sentences provide evidence of the coherence criterion.

*Lexical Resource*
This criterion refers to the ability to use a range of vocabulary and to express meanings and attitudes with precision.

The variety of words used, the adequacy and appropriacy of the words used, and the ability to overcome vocabulary gaps by using other words provide evidence of the lexical resource criterion.

*Grammatical Range and Accuracy*
This criterion refers to the ability to use a range of grammatical items accurately and appropriately.

The length and complexity of the spoken sentences, the appropriate use of subordinate clauses, and the range of structures used provide evidence of the grammatical range criterion.

The frequency of grammatical errors and the communicative effect of such errors provide evidence of the grammatical accuracy criterion.

*Pronunciation*
This criterion refers to the ability to use a range of phonological features consistently and accurately to convey meaning.

The intelligibility of sounds produced, the appropriate use of rhythm, stress and intonation, and the degree of effort required by the listener to understand what is being said provide evidence of the pronunciation criterion.

All criteria have equal weighting.

The public version of the Speaking band descriptors is available on the IELTS website **www.ielts.org**

# Sample Candidate Speaking Tests and Examiner Comments

On the CD included at the back of the booklet, you will find three candidate Speaking tests. Below, you will find examiner comments on each test and the Band Scores given.

The examiner guidelines for assessing candidate performance on the Speaking test are very detailed. There are many different ways a candidate may achieve a particular Band Score. The candidate performances on the CD should not be regarded as definitive examples of any particular Band Score.

## Speaking Test Example 1: Pakistani male
## Examiner Comments
### Band 7.5

The candidate speaks rapidly but fluently and his responses are relevant and well developed. He uses a sophisticated range of markers and cohesive devices. There is some repetition, but this has no effect on coherence. He uses a wide range of vocabulary with confidence and ease. There are many examples of precise idiomatic usage and good collocation. Inaccuracies are rare and minor. Overall, his control of grammar is a little weaker than other features of his performance. Though many sentences are correct, and he uses a wide range of sentence types, there are article and preposition problems and some verb form errors. These limit the rating for this criterion. He can be followed throughout the test, and he uses intonation and stress to good communicative effect. There are many examples of very natural speech. However, the speed of his speech, coupled with his strong accent, results in the marked pronunciation of some words. This is a high-level candidate whose variable grammatical control limits his rating to Band 7.5.

## Speaking Test Example 2: Thai female
## Examiner Comments
### Band 5

The candidate keeps going but she relies on strategies such as repetition and listing, and she has a slightly slow delivery. Some cohesive devices are used but she often resorts to 'yes' when she cannot complete an idea. Her sentences become disjointed at times and she loses fluency as her language becomes more complex. She manages to respond in all sections of the test and produces some adequate vocabulary. However, her limitations are apparent in her use of simple expressions, such as 'very nice' and 'something like that', and there is a lot of repetition. Despite attempts to use complex language, most of her sentences are simple. Some are incomplete and many contain errors. She uses mainly present tenses with noticeable omissions of articles and prepositions. There is occasional mispronunciation of words, such as 'clothes' and 'grammar', caused by her confusion/omission of individual sounds. Overall, however, she can be understood and she is beginning to use word stress and intonation to express her ideas. This candidate achieves a range of marks that result in an overall Band 5.

## Speaking Test Example 3: Iranian female
## Examiner Comments
### Band 6.5

The candidate gives long responses but she hesitates at times and repeatedly uses 'erm', which limits her fluency. She links her ideas using a range of connectors and markers but she uses some inaccurately. Her range of vocabulary is a strong feature of her interview, although her performance dips slightly in Part 2. She can use less common vocabulary, collocations and idiomatic expressions to good effect. However, there are examples of error and inappropriate word use. A range of sentence types is used and many of these are correct. She has good control of tenses and modal verbs. Conditionals are frequent and often accurate, and there are many examples of complex structures. However, there are some basic errors in preposition and pronoun use, as well as errors in word order. Her pronunciation is very clear but words are frequently over-pronounced and her speech is monotonous and jerky. Occasional confusion is caused by mispronunciation of words. The candidate has a strong lexical and structural base, but there is an effort involved in the way she speaks. This limits her rating to Band 6.5.

# Completing the Answer Sheets

Candidates are required to transfer their answers to an answer sheet for the Listening, Academic Reading and General Training Reading tests. The answer sheet is double-sided – one side for Listening and the other side for Reading. Ten minutes' extra time is allowed for transferring answers at the end of the Listening test. In the Reading test candidates are required to write their answers on the answer sheet during the time allowed for the test. **No extra time is allowed for transfer of the Reading answers.**

An example of a completed Listening answer sheet is given below. Please note the instructions for completing the answer sheet.

Candidates must take care when writing their answers on the answer sheet, as poor spelling and grammar are penalised.

After marking at the test centre, all answer sheets are returned to Cambridge ESOL for analysis.

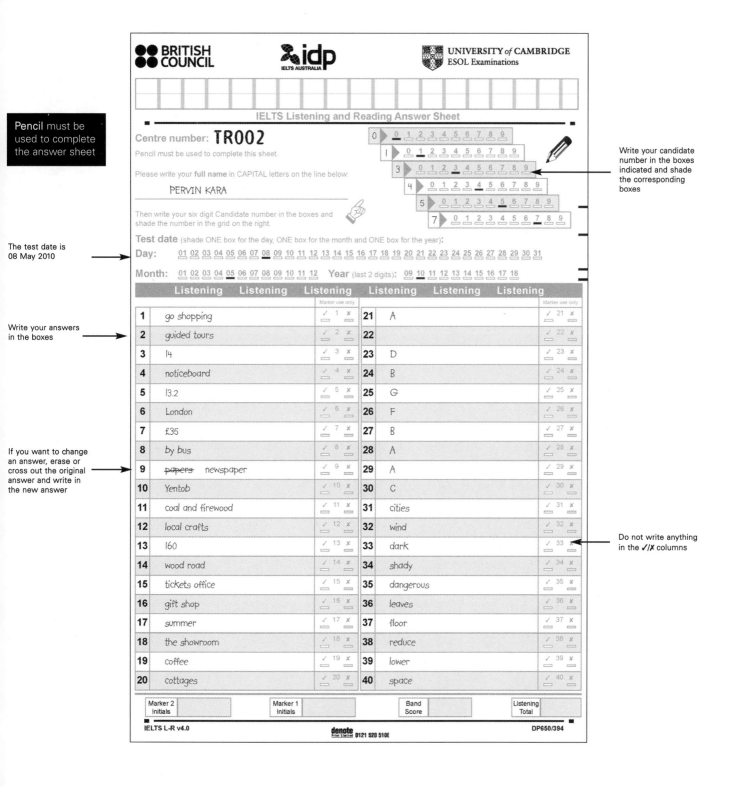

**Pencil** must be used to complete the answer sheet

The test date is 08 May 2010

Write your answers in the boxes

If you want to change an answer, erase or cross out the original answer and write in the new answer

Write your candidate number in the boxes indicated and shade the corresponding boxes

Do not write anything in the ✓/✗ columns

**IELTS Listening and Reading Answer Sheet**

Centre number: **TR002**

Please write your **full name** in CAPITAL letters on the line below:

PERVIN KARA

Then write your six digit Candidate number in the boxes and shade the number in the grid on the right.

**Test date** (shade ONE box for the day, ONE box for the month and ONE box for the year):

Day: 01 02 03 04 05 06 07 **08** 09 10 11 12 13 14 15 16 17 18 19 20 21 22 23 24 25 26 27 28 29 30 31

Month: 01 02 03 **04** 05 06 07 08 09 10 11 12    Year (last 2 digits): **09** 10 11 12 13 14 15 16 17 18

| # | Listening | # | Listening |
|---|---|---|---|
| 1 | go shopping | 21 | A |
| 2 | guided tours | 22 | |
| 3 | 14 | 23 | D |
| 4 | noticeboard | 24 | B |
| 5 | 13.2 | 25 | G |
| 6 | London | 26 | F |
| 7 | £35 | 27 | B |
| 8 | by bus | 28 | A |
| 9 | ~~papers~~ newspaper | 29 | A |
| 10 | Yentob | 30 | C |
| 11 | coal and firewood | 31 | cities |
| 12 | local crafts | 32 | wind |
| 13 | 160 | 33 | dark |
| 14 | wood road | 34 | shady |
| 15 | tickets office | 35 | dangerous |
| 16 | gift shop | 36 | leaves |
| 17 | summer | 37 | floor |
| 18 | the showroom | 38 | reduce |
| 19 | coffee | 39 | lower |
| 20 | cottages | 40 | space |

Marker 2 Initials    Marker 1 Initials    Band Score    Listening Total

IELTS L-R v4.0    denote Print Limited 0121 520 510(    DP650/394

# Listening Answer Sheet

## IELTS Listening and Reading Answer Sheet

**Centre number:**

Pencil must be used to complete this sheet.

0 1 2 3 4 5 6 7 8 9
0 1 2 3 4 5 6 7 8 9
0 1 2 3 4 5 6 7 8 9
0 1 2 3 4 5 6 7 8 9
0 1 2 3 4 5 6 7 8 9
0 1 2 3 4 5 6 7 8 9

Please write your **full name** in CAPITAL letters on the line below:

SAMPLE

Then write your six digit Candidate number in the boxes and shade the number in the grid on the right.

**Test date** (shade ONE box for the day, ONE box for the month and ONE box for the year):

**Day:** 01 02 03 04 05 06 07 08 09 10 11 12 13 14 15 16 17 18 19 20 21 22 23 24 25 26 27 28 29 30 31

**Month:** 01 02 03 04 05 06 07 08 09 10 11 12    **Year** (last 2 digits): 09 10 11 12 13 14 15 16 17 18

| | Listening    Listening    Listening | Marker use only | | Listening    Listening    Listening | Marker use only |
|---|---|---|---|---|---|
| 1 | | ✓ 1 ✗ | 21 | | ✓ 21 ✗ |
| 2 | | ✓ 2 ✗ | 22 | | ✓ 22 ✗ |
| 3 | | ✓ 3 ✗ | 23 | | ✓ 23 ✗ |
| 4 | | ✓ 4 ✗ | 24 | | ✓ 24 ✗ |
| 5 | | ✓ 5 ✗ | 25 | | ✓ 25 ✗ |
| 6 | | ✓ 6 ✗ | 26 | | ✓ 26 ✗ |
| 7 | | ✓ 7 ✗ | 27 | | ✓ 27 ✗ |
| 8 | | ✓ 8 ✗ | 28 | | ✓ 28 ✗ |
| 9 | | ✓ 9 ✗ | 29 | | ✓ 29 ✗ |
| 10 | | ✓ 10 ✗ | 30 | | ✓ 30 ✗ |
| 11 | | ✓ 11 ✗ | 31 | | ✓ 31 ✗ |
| 12 | | ✓ 12 ✗ | 32 | | ✓ 32 ✗ |
| 13 | | ✓ 13 ✗ | 33 | | ✓ 33 ✗ |
| 14 | | ✓ 14 ✗ | 34 | | ✓ 34 ✗ |
| 15 | | ✓ 15 ✗ | 35 | | ✓ 35 ✗ |
| 16 | | ✓ 16 ✗ | 36 | | ✓ 36 ✗ |
| 17 | | ✓ 17 ✗ | 37 | | ✓ 37 ✗ |
| 18 | | ✓ 18 ✗ | 38 | | ✓ 38 ✗ |
| 19 | | ✓ 19 ✗ | 39 | | ✓ 39 ✗ |
| 20 | | ✓ 20 ✗ | 40 | | ✓ 40 ✗ |

| Marker 2 Initials | | Marker 1 Initials | | Band Score | | Listening Total | |
|---|---|---|---|---|---|---|---|

# Academic/General Training Reading Answer Sheet

Please write your **full name** in CAPITAL letters on the line below:

SAMPLE

Please write your Candidate number on the line below:

_____

Please write your three digit language code in the boxes and shade the numbers in the grid on the right.

0 1 2 3 4 5 6 7 8 9
0 1 2 3 4 5 6 7 8 9
0 1 2 3 4 5 6 7 8 9

**Are you:** Female? ⬜  Male? ⬜

| Reading Reading Reading Reading Reading Reading |

**Module taken** (shade one box): Academic ⬜   General Training ⬜

| | | Marker use only | | | | Marker use only |
|---|---|---|---|---|---|---|
| 1 | | ✓ 1 ✗ | 21 | | | ✓ 21 ✗ |
| 2 | | ✓ 2 ✗ | 22 | | | ✓ 22 ✗ |
| 3 | | ✓ 3 ✗ | 23 | | | ✓ 23 ✗ |
| 4 | | ✓ 4 ✗ | 24 | | | ✓ 24 ✗ |
| 5 | | ✓ 5 ✗ | 25 | | | ✓ 25 ✗ |
| 6 | | ✓ 6 ✗ | 26 | | | ✓ 26 ✗ |
| 7 | | ✓ 7 ✗ | 27 | | | ✓ 27 ✗ |
| 8 | | ✓ 8 ✗ | 28 | | | ✓ 28 ✗ |
| 9 | | ✓ 9 ✗ | 29 | | | ✓ 29 ✗ |
| 10 | | ✓ 10 ✗ | 30 | | | ✓ 30 ✗ |
| 11 | | ✓ 11 ✗ | 31 | | | ✓ 31 ✗ |
| 12 | | ✓ 12 ✗ | 32 | | | ✓ 32 ✗ |
| 13 | | ✓ 13 ✗ | 33 | | | ✓ 33 ✗ |
| 14 | | ✓ 14 ✗ | 34 | | | ✓ 34 ✗ |
| 15 | | ✓ 15 ✗ | 35 | | | ✓ 35 ✗ |
| 16 | | ✓ 16 ✗ | 36 | | | ✓ 36 ✗ |
| 17 | | ✓ 17 ✗ | 37 | | | ✓ 37 ✗ |
| 18 | | ✓ 18 ✗ | 38 | | | ✓ 38 ✗ |
| 19 | | ✓ 19 ✗ | 39 | | | ✓ 39 ✗ |
| 20 | | ✓ 20 ✗ | 40 | | | ✓ 40 ✗ |

| Marker 2 Initials | | Marker 1 Initials | | Band Score | | Reading Total | |
|---|---|---|---|---|---|---|---|

# Academic/General Training Writing Answer Booklet

## INTERNATIONAL ENGLISH LANGUAGE TESTING SYSTEM

**BRITISH COUNCIL**　　**idp** IELTS AUSTRALIA　　**UNIVERSITY** *of* **CAMBRIDGE**
ESOL Examinations

### WRITING ANSWER BOOKLET

Candidate Name: ...........................................　　Candidate Number: ..................................................

Centre Number: ...........................................　　Date: ....................................................................

Module:　ACADEMIC ☐　　GENERAL TRAINING ☐　　(Tick as appropriate)

### TASK 1

_____

_____

_____

_____

_____

_____

_____

_____

_____

_____

_____

_____

EXAMINER'S USE ONLY

EXAMINER 2 NUMBER: .........................................

CANDIDATE NUMBER: ..........................................　　EXAMINER 1 NUMBER: .........................................

EXAMINER'S USE ONLY

| EXAMINER 2 TASK 1 | TA | | CC | | LR | | GRA | |
|---|---|---|---|---|---|---|---|---|

| UNDERLENGTH | | NO OF WORDS | | PENALTY | |
|---|---|---|---|---|---|
| OFF-TOPIC | | MEMORISED | | ILLEGIBLE | |

| EXAMINER 1 TASK 1 | TA | | CC | | LR | | GRA | |
|---|---|---|---|---|---|---|---|---|

| UNDERLENGTH | | NO OF WORDS | | PENALTY | |
|---|---|---|---|---|---|
| OFF-TOPIC | | MEMORISED | | ILLEGIBLE | |

EXAMINER'S USE ONLY

_____

_____

_____

_____

_____

_____

_____

_____

_____

_____

_____

_____

_____

_____

_____

_____

_____

_____

_____

_____

_____

_____

_____

_____

_____

| EXAMINER'S USE ONLY |
|---|

| EXAMINER 2 TASK 2 | TR | | CC | | LR | | GRA | |
|---|---|---|---|---|---|---|---|---|

| UNDERLENGTH | | NO OF WORDS | | PENALTY | |
|---|---|---|---|---|---|
| OFF-TOPIC | | MEMORISED | | ILLEGIBLE | |

| EXAMINER 1 TASK 2 | TR | | CC | | LR | | GRA | |
|---|---|---|---|---|---|---|---|---|

| UNDERLENGTH | | NO OF WORDS | | PENALTY | |
|---|---|---|---|---|---|
| OFF-TOPIC | | MEMORISED | | ILLEGIBLE | |